The Bible Speaks Today

Series Editors: J. A. Motyer (OT)
John R. W. Stott (NT)

Songs from a Strange Land,
The Message of Psalms 42–51, John Goldingay

A Time to Mourn, and a Time to Dance,
The Message of Ecclesiastes, Derek Kidner

The Lord Is King,
The Message of Daniel, Ronald S. Wallace

The Day of the Lion,
The Message of Amos, J. A. Motyer

Christian Counter-Culture,
The Message of the Sermon on the Mount, John R. W. Stott

The Savior of the World,
The Message of Luke's Gospel, Michael Wilcock

Only One Way,
The Message of Galatians, John R. W. Stott

God's New Society,
The Message of Ephesians, John R. W. Stott

Fullness and Freedom,
The Message of Colossians and Philemon, R. C. Lucas

Guard the Gospel,
The Message of 2 Timothy, John R. W. Stott

I Saw Heaven Opened,
The Message of Revelation, Michael Wilcock

A TIME TO MOURN & A TIME TO DANCE

The Message of Ecclesiastes

THE BIBLE SPEAKS TODAY

Derek Kidner

InterVarsity Press
Downers Grove
Illinois 60515

© 1976 by Inter-Varsity Press, Leicester, England

Printed in America by InterVarsity Press, Downers Grove, Illinois, with permission from Universities and Colleges Christian Fellowship, Leicester, England.

InterVarsity Press is the book-publishing division of Inter-Varsity Christian Fellowship, a student movement active on campus at hundreds of universities, colleges and schools of nursing. For information about local and regional activities, write IVCF, 233 Langdon St., Madison, WI 53703.

Distributed in Canada through InterVarsity Press, 1875 Leslie St., Unit 10, Don Mills, Ontario M3B 2M5, Canada.

The Bible text in this publication is from the Revised Standard Version, copyrighted 1952 by the Division of Christian Education, National Council of the Churches of Christ in the United States of America, and used by permission.

ISBN 0-87784-647-2
Library of Congress Catalog Card Number: 76-21460

Printed in the United States of America

General Preface

The Bible speaks today describes a projected series of both Old and New Testament expositions, which are characterized by a threefold ideal: to expound the biblical text with accuracy, to relate it to contemporary life, and to be readable.

These books are, therefore, not 'commentaries', for the commentary seeks rather to elucidate the text than to apply it, and tends to be a work rather of reference than of literature. Nor, on the other hand, do they contain the kind of 'sermons' which attempt to be contemporary and readable, without taking Scripture seriously enough.

The contributors to this series will all be united in their convictions that God still speaks through what He has spoken, and that nothing is more necessary for the life, growth and health of churches or of Christians than that they should hear and heed what the Spirit is saying to them through His ancient—yet ever modern—Word.

J. A. MOTYER
J. R. W. STOTT
Series Editors

Contents

General Preface
Author's Preface
Chief Abbreviations

Part One: What is this book doing in the Bible?
　—a reconnaissance　　　　　　　　　　　　　　　　　　13

Part Two: What is the book saying?
　—a running commentary　　　　　　　　　　　　　　　21
The author, the motto and a survey of the scene 1:1-11　21
The search for satisfaction 1:12—2:26　　　　　　　　28
The tyranny of time 3:1-15　　　　　　　　　　　　　37
The harshness of life 3:16—4:3　　　　　　　　　　　41
The rat-race 4:4-8　　　　　　　　　　　　　　　　45
A first summary:
A backward glance over Ecclesiastes 1:1—4:8　　　　48

Interlude:
Some reflections, maxims and home truths 4:9—5:12　50

The bitterness of disappointment 5:13—6:12　　　　57

A second summary:
A backward glance over Ecclesiastes 4:9—6:12　　　63

Interlude:
More reflections, maxims and home truths 7:1-22　　64

The search goes on 7:23-29　　　　　　　　　　　　71
Frustration 8:1-17　　　　　　　　　　　　　　　　74
Jeopardy 9:1-18　　　　　　　　　　　　　　　　　80

A third summary:
A backward glance over Ecclesiastes 7:1—9:18   86

Interlude:
Be sensible! 10:1–20   88

Towards home 11:1—12:8   96
Conclusion 12:9–14   10)

Part Three: What are we to say to this?
    —an epilogue   109

Author's Preface

ANYONE who spends time with Ecclesiastes (that least ecclesiastical of men) finds himself in the company of a highly independent and fascinating mind. This leads me to say two things.

First, to express thanks to the editor of this series for giving me the excuse to study the book more closely than before.

Secondly, to suggest that some readers may do well to go straight to Part Two, the running commentary, where they can hear the Preacher himself—admittedly with interruptions from me—without waiting for the survey which is attempted in Part One. It depends on whether one prefers to have things mapped out in advance, or to plunge in and feel one's way along.

Either way, may it be a journey home.

Tyndale House,
Cambridge

DEREK KIDNER

Chief Abbreviations

ANET	*Ancient Near Eastern Texts* by J. B. Pritchard (2nd ed., OUP, 1955).
AV	English Authorized Version (King James), 1611.
Barton	*Ecclesiastes* by G. A. Barton (*International Critical Commentary*, T. & T. Clark, 1908).
Delitzsch	*The Song of Songs and Ecclesiastes* by F. Delitzsch (T. & T. Clark, 1891).
Gk.	Greek.
Heb.	Hebrew.
JB	The Jerusalem Bible, 1966.
Jones	*Proverbs, Ecclesiastes* by E. Jones (*Torch Bible Commentaries*, SCM Press, 1961).
LXX	The Septuagint (pre-Christian Greek version of the Old Testament).
McNeile	*An Introduction to Ecclesiastes* by A. H. McNeile (CUP, 1904).
mg.	margin.
MS(S)	manuscript(s).
MT	Massoretic Text.
NEB	The New English Bible, Old Testament, 1970.
RSV	American Revised Standard Version, 1946–52.
RV	English Revised Version, 1881–84.
Scott	*Proverbs, Ecclesiastes* by R. B. Y. Scott (*Anchor Bible*, Doubleday, 1965).
TEV	Today's English Version, Proverbs and Ecclesiastes: *Wisdom for Modern Man* (American Bible Society, 1972).

Part One
WHAT IS THIS BOOK DOING IN THE BIBLE?
—a reconnaissance

THE voice of the Old Testament has many accents. There is almost everything there, from the impassioned preaching of the prophets to the cool, reflective comments of the wise—and a whole world of poetry, law, story-telling, psalmody and vision in between.

But there is no-one quite like Qoheleth[1] (to give him his untranslatable title); no book in this whole great volume which speaks in quite his tone of voice.

His natural habitat, so to speak, is among the wise men who teach us to use our eyes as well as our ears to learn the ways of God and man. Some of his sayings could have come straight out of Proverbs, and he has a way of pausing to steady us and give us our bearings by this homely wisdom, at intervals between our more unsettling excursions with him. Wisdom—quite practical and orthodox—is his base-camp; but he is an explorer. His concern is with the boundaries of life, and especially with the questions that most of us would hesitate to push too far.

His probing is so relentless that he can easily be taken for a sceptic or a pessimist. His opening cry, 'Vanity of vanities!', or 'Utter futility!', almost asks for it; but there is more to him than

[1] Pronounced Ko-*hell*eth or Ko-*hell*et. The word is connected with the Hebrew for assembling, and its form suggests some kind of office-bearer. This status was possibly academic (a collector or assembler of sayings?—*cf.* 12:9 ff., where, however, other words are used for this activity), or more probably ecclesiastical (as convenor of the assembly, or the one who addresses it?), since the standard word for the congregation or church shares the same root as this. The many attempts at translating this title include: 'Ecclesiastes', 'The Preacher', 'The Speaker', 'The President', 'The Spokesman', 'The Philosopher'. We might almost add, 'The Professor'!

PART ONE—A RECONNAISSANCE

can be captured in a phrase, even a motto-phrase. So much more, in fact, that at one time there were scholars ready to suggest that two, or three, or even as many as nine[2] different minds had been at work on the book. Such are its cross-currents and swift changes; but they can all be seen as the insights of a single mind, approaching the facts of life and death from a variety of angles.

At bottom we can find the axiom of all the wise men of the Bible, that the fear of the Lord is the beginning of wisdom. But Qoheleth plans to bring us to that point last of all, when we are desperate for an answer. There are hints of it in passing, but his main approach is from the other end: the resolve to see how far a man will get with no such basis. He puts himself—and us—in the shoes of the humanist or secularist. Not the atheist, for atheism was hardly a going concern in his day, but the person who starts his thinking from man and the observable world, and knows God only from a distance.

This of course is asking for complications. There will be tension between the writer's deepest self, as a man of conviction with a faith to share, and his provisional self as a man groping his way by the light of nature. And this second self has its own conflicts, familiar to us all, between the voices of conscience, self-interest and experience, and between God as we acknowledge Him and God as we treat Him.

Once we see what is broadly happening in the book, it is not too difficult to find our way about it; and the running commentary may provide some further help. Meanwhile it may be useful to bring together some of the teachings that are scattered through its pages, and look for the general thrust of the argument.

Facts to face about God

If one believes in God at all, the implications deserve to be followed right through. Qoheleth expects us to do this, and not to imagine that we can take liberties with our Maker or manipulate Him in our interests. We are confronted with God at His most formidable: as one who is not impressed by our chatter or by our ritual gifts and airy promises. The opening paragraphs of chapter 5 drive home these points with vigour. 'God is in heaven, and

[2] So D. C. Siegfried, 'Prediger und Hohelied', in W. Nowack, *Handkommentar zum Alten Testament* (Göttingen, 1898).

you upon earth; therefore let your words be few. . . He has no pleasure in fools.'

God meets us in this book in three main aspects: as Creator, as Sovereign, and as Unsearchable Wisdom. Not that any of these actual terms are used of Him, except the first; but they may serve as a convenient focus.

As *Creator*, He sets the whole scene. We are reminded that His world has its own obstinate shape which we cannot iron out to our liking (which therefore, incidentally, has a certain built-in resistance, mercifully enough, to us as planners and standard-izers[3]); for 'who can make straight what he has made crooked?' (7:13). It also has its own inexorable rhythm in which we find ourselves caught up: a time for this and a time for that, with very little choice for us in the matter, as chapter 3 points out. Even as procreators we do no more than activate the mysterious process in which God brings into being a new life. 'As you do not know how the spirit comes to the bones in the womb of a woman with child, so you do not know the work of God *who makes everything*' (11:5).

But we are not allowed the luxury of blaming the Creator for our tangles and misdeeds, as the Babylonian Theodicy blames the gods,[4] for 'God made man straightforward'. The responsibility is put where it belongs, in the sequel to that remark: 'but man invents endless subtleties' (7:29, NEB).

As *Sovereign*, however, it is God who has prescribed the frustrations we find in life. The treadmill of existence which is pictured at the very outset of the book (surely Qoheleth, by the way, would have had a wry smile for the show-title, 'Stop the world, I want to get off!')—that treadmill is God's appointment. 'It is an unhappy business that *God has given* to the sons of men to be busy with . . . All is vanity and a striving after wind' (1:13, 14). True, there is a hint of the fall of man which gave the occasion for that decree, in the saying of 7:29 which we have just looked at. True again, Paul in Romans 8:18–25 would take up this picture of 'the creation . . . subjected to futility', to show the forward thrust it generates. But the emphasis of Ecclesiastes is on what never seems to change, and on the disappointments we live with here and now.

[3] *Cf.* 11:1–6.
[4] See the comment on 7:29.

All of this comes from God: the general web of life and its minutest strands, whether these are to our liking and our sense of what is fitting, or not. Sometimes they will make sense to us, for as a rule the sinner comes in for an extra dose of frustration through God's care for His own (2:26); but it remains a fact that nothing whatever is ours to command or to count on. If the sinner is tantalized, he is not the only one. Tragedy can strike anybody, and God will be behind it. Chapter 6:1–6 is one of the places where this is faced: it makes the point that the more you feel entitled to, and the more you have already, the harder it will seem if God withdraws it, as He may at any moment (6:2 ff.), and as He ultimately will. For 'do not all go to the one place?' (6b)—that is, to the grave.

So we are driven to face the hiddenness of God's ways. In terms of our three titles for Him, He meets us now as *Unsearchable Wisdom*, reducing our most brilliant thoughts to little more than guesses.

The place where this is put to us most gracefully and with most promise is 3:11, one of the unexpected summits of the book. 'He has made everything beautiful in its time; also he has put eternity into man's mind, yet so that he cannot find out what God has done from the beginning to the end.' This single sentence captures the dazzling, bewildering beauty of a world so changeful that its total pattern is beyond us. But pattern it is. We, unlike the animals, can grasp enough to be sure of that, yet never enough to see the whole.

One consequence is that we cannot extrapolate from the present. Whether things are going well or ill, we have to take them as they come, knowing that the whole picture will change and go on changing. 'God has made the one as well as the other'—good times and bad—'so that man may not find out anything that will be after him' (7:14).

Obviously the future is as hidden as this. What is not so obvious is that the present, which does lie open to our inspection, eludes us as well. It belongs, just as much as the future, to God. 'Then I saw all the work of God, that man cannot find out the work that is done under the sun' (8:17)—cannot fathom, in other words, the ordinary activities all about him. 'However much man may toil in seeking,' Qoheleth continues, 'he will not find it out.' Philosophies will be constructed, but every one of them will be found wanting: 'even though a wise man claims to know, he cannot find it out.' It is hauntingly expressed in 7:23, 24: 'I said, "I will be wise"; but it was far from me. That which is, is far off, and deep, very deep; who can find it out?'

This obscurity is intellectually teasing; yet we can enjoy a good problem as a mental exercise. It is quite another matter if we are left guessing whether the universe—indeed, whether God —is hostile or not. But that is exactly what we cannot find out for ourselves, or take any steps to control. This seems to be the meaning of 9:1, which speaks of being 'in the hand of God'. But what kind of God? To the man who knows the God of Israel, nothing could sound more reassuring; but to the person groping for the meaning of life it is a paralysing thought. 'Whether it is love or hate man does not know.' Is he to go by the delights of nature or by its ruthlessness? By the smiles of fortune or by its frowns—which no amount of good living or good management can control with any certainty?

This brings us to the other plane on which we are invited to look at life.

Facts to face from experience

One of the most fascinating passages in the book is a tour of exploration into the rewards and satisfactions of experience.[5] With Qoheleth we put on the mantle of a Solomon, that most brilliant and least limited of men, to set out on the search. With every gift and power at our command, it would be strange if we should come back empty-handed.

We start with wisdom—the most promising of pursuits. But in a disordered world 'he who increases knowledge increases sorrow' (1:18) by the very clarity of his insight. And in the last analysis, whatever else wisdom can do for one, it can do nothing about the end of life. In that crisis the wise man is as naked as the fool (2:15–17)—and if his wisdom counts for nothing at that point, it is a pretentious failure.

So we swing to 'madness and folly' (1:17; 2:3b)—and this has a modern ring, chiming in with some of our attempts to by-pass the rational by exploring the absurd and the world of hallucinations. Pleasure, of course, is yet another realm: a many-sided one with its appeal to sensual appetites at one end of the scale (2:3,

[5] See the much fuller comments on this passage (1:16—2:26), on pp. 30–36.

8c), and the aesthetic joys of the connoisseur and the creative worker at the other.

Even the best of these pursuits, though, will satisfy us only in passing. There comes the reckoning—'Then I considered all that my hands had done' (2:11)—and because of death the final count comes out at nothing. What makes it still more painful is to realize that this zero-result is an obliteration, an undoing. There *are* values: 'wisdom excels folly as light excels darkness' (2:13); but there are none that endure when we are no longer there— nor anyone else—to value them.

The second obstinate fact is that of evil. It is as tyrannous as death itself, and even more tragic. The impermanence of life is sad enough, but its wrongs can be unbearable.

Qoheleth has an eye for the mean sins as well as the massive ones: the envy that inspires or else attends success (4:4); the money-fixation that makes the lonely tycoon a pathetic and point- less figure (4:7, 8); the vanity that sustains a fool too long in office (4:13), to name but a few. But chiefly he mourns 'the oppressions that are practised under the sun' (4:1). 'In the place of justice, even there was wickedness' (3:16). 'On the side of . . . oppressors there was power' (4:1). The very structures of society contribute to these things (5:8), but they are diseases not simply of official- dom but of humanity. 'There is not a righteous man on earth' (7:20); indeed, 'the hearts of men are full of evil, and madness is in their hearts while they live' (9:3). The reader can reflect on the collective insanity which visibly takes hold of a society from time to time—but also on that madness which may be invisible because he shares it as the climate of his age.

On top of all this, as if death and evil were not enough, there is the smaller but equally unmanageable factor of 'time and chance' to reckon with (9:11). The well-organized man may bask in self-sufficiency, but Qoheleth sees through it. It is self- deception. Even the most limited and predictable prizes in life— let alone the quest for something ultimate—can go astray, and a man be left with nothing. 'The race is not to the swift, nor the battle to the strong'—not, that is, with any certainty. 'For man does not know his time' (9:12). He can pretend he does; but pretence is no basis for life. We are reminded of the dismissive comment on the man who had thought of everything but this. 'God said to him, "You fool! . . .".'

Down to bed-rock

If there is little left after this analysis, it is exactly what the writer intends—but only as his preliminary work. He is demolishing to build. The searching questions he has asked are those that life itself puts to us, if we will only listen. He can afford to ask them, because in the final chapters he has good news for us, once we can stop pretending that what is mortal is enough for us, who have been given a capacity for the eternal.

It is news, paradoxically, of judgment.

To make that paradox a little clearer, it may help if we digress for a while, to look at an old example of thoroughgoing secularism, softened by none of our modern utopian fancies, and stiffened by no sense of anything transcendent: only by its own cool detachment and wit. The passage, for the most part very freely paraphrased and sampled here, is the Mesopotamian dialogue between master and servant, written perhaps before the time of Moses.[6]

> 'Servant, obey me.' 'Yes, my lord, yes.'
> 'The chariot—hitch it up. I will ride to the palace.'
> 'Ride, my lord, ride! . . . The king will be gracious to you.'
> 'No, servant, I shall not ride to the palace.'
> 'Don't ride, my lord, don't ride. The king might send you to some outlandish place. You'd never get a moment's peace.'

Next it takes his fancy to dine—which the servant greets with suitable remarks. There's nothing so agreeable and soothing, is there? But the fancy passes: he will not dine after all. The servant finds this very fitting: there's nothing quite so commonplace as eating, is there?

So it goes on. He will go hunting . . .; but no, he decides against it. Or he will lead a rebellion—or refrain from it. Preserve a crushing silence when he meets his rival . . . Better still, speak out at him. Every idea is capped by some admiring remark from the servant, and every opposite idea is even sounder sense.

Soon he feels in the mood for love (ah yes! nothing like it, sir, for taking your mind off things); and then he doesn't (how wise! woman is a pitfall, a dagger at your throat). Now he has it! He will be a philanthropist. Yet on the other hand . . . (right again,

[6] Translated in, e.g., *ANET*, p. 438.

sir; what good would it have done you? Ask the skulls in the graveyard!).

In this fatuous, idle mood, thought after thought, value after value, is picked up, turned on its head and tossed away. In the end, the gentleman toys with a serious question. 'What is good?' His own answer gives us a jolt: 'To break my neck, your neck, throw both in the river—that is good.' Of course he changes his mind: he will just break his servant's neck, send him on ahead.

Predictably the servant gets the last word. How would his lord survive for even three days—with no-one to look after him?

Now we can make too much of this talk of ending it all by a death pact. It makes an effective curtain to the comedy. Yet it may speak more truly than it knows: for when you learn to laugh at everything you are soon left with nothing worth the bother of a laugh. Triviality is more stifling than tragedy, and the shrug is the most hopeless of all comments on life.

The function of Ecclesiastes is to bring us to the point where we begin to fear that such a comment is the only honest one. So it is, if everything is dying. We face the appalling inference that nothing has meaning, nothing matters under the sun. It is then that we can hear, as the good news which it is, that *everything* matters—'for God will bring every deed into judgment, with every secret thing, whether good or evil.'

That is how the book will end. On this rock we can be destroyed: but it is rock, not quicksand. There is the chance to build.

Part Two
WHAT IS THE BOOK SAYING?
—a running commentary

Ecclesiastes 1:1—11
The author, the motto
and a survey of the scene

Introducing the author

1:1 *The words of the Preacher, the son of David, king in Jerusalem.*

There is a certain mystery about this writer's way of announcing himself; and this intriguing touch is not likely to be unintentional. First, he comes almost but not quite to the point of calling himself Solomon. That name never occurs in the book; yet Proverbs and the Song of Songs use it openly in claiming him as their author. Then there is the curious double title, ecclesiastical and royal[1]—almost as if one were to speak of 'The Vicar, King of England'! There will be another enigmatic note in verse 16, with its claim to a wisdom 'surpassing all who were over Jerusalem before me'. This rules out any successor to the matchless Solomon, but almost equally Solomon himself, who had only one Israelite predecessor there.[2]

When we add to this the fact that all the signs of royalty will fade after the first two chapters,[3] it seems fairly clear that we are

[1] See the footnote on p. 13 for the meaning of Qoheleth ('The Preacher').
[2] Also the sense of long retrospect in that phrase seems borne out by the apparently late form of Hebrew in this book, which seems to be at a half-way stage between classical and rabbinic Hebrew. This is not conclusive, however, since it can be argued that many of its features are those of Phoenician dialect, not of date. See the discussions of this by M. J. Dahood in *Biblica* 33 (1952), pp. 32–52 and 191–221; also in *Biblica* 39 (1958), pp. 302–318; and by G. L. Archer in *Bulletin of the Evangelical Theological Society* 12 (1969), pp. 167–181. The latter argues for Solomon's authorship, drawing attention to his close links with the Phoenicians.
[3] Only the title Qoheleth ('The Preacher') will be used after this (7:27; 12:8–10), and the writer's stance becomes that of a mere observer, not a ruler. See, *e.g.*, 3:16; 4:1–3; 5:8 f.

meant to see the non-royal title as the writer's own, and the royal one as simply a means of dramatizing the quest he describes in chapters one and two. He pictures for us a super-Solomon (as he implies by the word 'surpassing', in 1:16) to demonstrate that the most gifted man conceivable, who could outstrip every king who ever occupied the throne of David, would still return empty-handed from the quest for self-fulfilment.[4]

From the fuller account of the author in 12:9 f. we have the portrait of a scholar whose vocation is teaching, research, editing and creative writing. What his book as a whole tells us indirectly is that he is as sensitive as he is courageous, and a master of style.

The motto

1:2 *Vanity of vanities, says the Preacher,*
vanity of vanities! All is vanity.

A wisp of vapour, a puff of wind, a mere breath—nothing you could get your hands on; the nearest thing to zero. That is the 'vanity' this book is about.

What makes this reading of life disturbing is that this airy nothingness is not seen as a mere flicker on the surface of things, where it might even have had a certain charm. It is the sum total.

If that is really so—and the rest of the book will be arguing that it is—it makes 'vanity' a desperate word. It will no longer mean simply what is slight and passing, but more ominously, what is pointless. The author doubles and redoubles this bitter word, using twice over a phrase which might be a parody of that other superlative, 'holy of holies'. Utter emptiness stands here in mute contrast to utter holiness, that potent reality which gave shape and point to the traditional piety of Israel. Finally he clinches it with the terse dismissal, 'All is vanity.' In the terms we use today the summing up could be:

'Utter futility . . ., utter futility!
The whole thing is futile.'

But what is this 'whole thing'? Does it include godliness—and God? Or is it everything short of this?

The author is in no hurry to answer. He wants us to look very

[4] See also the comment and footnote at 1:12 (p. 28).

closely at the world we can see and at the answers it seems to give, before he will do more than drop hints of his own standpoint. The first of these quiet hints, however, comes immediately, in the phrase *under the sun* (1:3), which will become something of a keynote to the book, reiterated nearly thirty times in its twelve short chapters. Unless it is no more than a mannerism—but this author does not waste words—it makes it clear enough that the scene in mind is exclusively the world we can observe, and that our observation point is at ground level.

In that case, not only the cry, 'Vanity of vanities!' but all the comments on life that will chime in with it, already have their boundaries, their frame of reference, sketched in by that phrase. At the end of the book the lines will be quite firmly drawn, and Qoheleth revealed as a man of faith. Meanwhile they are put in with the lightest touch, and their implications wait to be discovered. We may traditionally call this man 'the Preacher', but he stands so close to his audience that his words might seem to them the embodiment of their most radical thoughts. Where he differs from them is in following such trains of thought much further than they would care to take them. Path after path will be relentlessly explored to the very point at which it comes to nothing. In the end, only one way will be left.

The process has been so admirably described by G. S. Hendry that it would be a pity not to quote him at this point:

'Qoheleth writes from concealed premises, and his book is in reality a major work of apologetic . . . . Its apparent worldliness is dictated by its aim: Qoheleth is addressing the general public whose view is bounded by the horizons of this world; he meets them on their own ground, and proceeds to convict them of its inherent vanity. This is further borne out by his characteristic expression "under the sun", by which he describes what the NT calls "the world" . . . . His book is in fact a critique of secularism and of secularized religion.'[5]

The treadmill

1:3 *What does man gain by all the toil*
at which he toils under the sun?

[5] G. S. Hendry, Introduction to article 'Ecclesiastes', in *The New Bible Commentary Revised* (IVP, 1970), p. 570.

> [4] *A generation goes, and a generation comes,*
>   *but the earth remains for ever.*
> [5] *The sun rises and the sun goes down,*
>   *and hastens to the place where it rises.*
> [6] *The wind blows to the south,*
>   *and goes round to the north;*
> *round and round goes the wind,*
>   *and on its circuits the wind returns.*
> [7] *All streams run to the sea,*
>   *but the sea is not full;*
> *to the place where the streams flow,*
>   *there they flow again.*
> [8] *All things are full of weariness;*
>   *a man cannot utter it;*
> *the eye is not satisfied with seeing,*
>   *nor the ear filled with hearing.*
> [9] *What has been is what will be,*
>   *and what has been done is what will be done;*
>   *and there is nothing new under the sun.*
> [10] *Is there a thing of which it is said,*
>   *'See, this is new'?*
> *It has been already,*
>   *in the ages before us.*
> [11] *There is no remembrance of former things,*
>   *nor will there be any remembrance*
> *of later things yet to happen*
>   *among those who come after.*

We have already stolen a glance at this passage to notice the phrase 'under the sun', which sets the scene for the book as a whole. True to that opening, this sequence looks at life within those mundane limits which are the same for all men.

What does man gain . . .? It is a hard-headed question and a characteristic one. This particular word for *gain*, drawn from the world of business, is native to this book alone in Scripture.[6] But before we write it off as cynical or mercenary we have to remember the comparable question in the Gospel: 'What does it profit a man . . .?'[7] This is not the only place where Christ and

[6] *Cf.* the Heb. text of 2:11, 13, 13; 3:9; 5:9, 16 (Heb. 8, 15); 7:12; 10:10, 11.

[7] Mk. 8:36.

24

Qoheleth speak the same language. It is a fair question. Any
romantic appeal that a hopeless venture may have for us would
soon evaporate if no other kind of venture existed—and where
is the proof that in the long run there will be any other kind?
'You spend your life working, labouring, and what do you have
to show for it?'—so runs a free translation of this verse.[8]

Ah, but one hopes to make the world a better place, or at least
leave something for those who follow. As though expecting that
reply, Qoheleth points to the ceaseless making and unmaking that
goes on in human history: the wave after wave of generations
with their rise and fall, their coming men who are soon forgotten
men; all this against the impassive background of the earth,
which sees each generation out and goes on for ever. No doubt
it will see the last of us off the scene, and what will man amount
to then?

Besides, the world's own pattern, however long the earth remains, is as restless and repetitive as ours. So many fine beginnings double back. So many journeys end where they began.
Qoheleth picks out three examples of this endless round in nature,
starting with the most obvious, that of the sun, which stoops
from its great upward curve into its decline; and having done so,
hastens [9] to repeat itself day after day. His other two examples
may seem at first to offer some escape from circularity—for what
is freer than the wind, or less reversible than a torrent? But
follow the process far enough and you come back to the beginning. The winds go 'round and round'; the waters, as Job 36:27
f. points out, are drawn up again to shower down on the earth
as before. So the very regularities of the world which may speak
to us, on God's behalf, of mercies 'new every morning', will give
a very different answer if we look for meaning from them in themselves. Verse 8 sums up their perpetual circling as unutterable
weariness.[1]

All this holds up a mirror to the human scene. Like the ocean,

[8] I:3, TEV.
[9] The word *hastens* (5) is lit. 'pants'—whether from eagerness or weariness
the author refrains from saying. Elsewhere it mostly has an eager ring (*e.g.*,
Jb. 5:5; 7:2; Ps. 119:131), but the context is sombre (*cf.* verse 8) and the word
can indicate distress (Is. 42:14).
[1] Another translation of verse 8a, favoured by some commentators, is 'All
words are feeble' (RV mg.), *i.e.*, 'the scene is beyond description'. But the adjective elsewhere means 'weary' (Dt. 25:18; 2 Sa. 17:2) and the passage as a
whole is emphasizing not the complexity but the unremitting round of nature.

our senses are fed and fed, but never filled. And like the wheel of nature, our history is always turning back on itself, failing of its promise. The journey goes on; we never arrive. Under the sun there is nowhere to make for, nothing finally satisfying or really new. As for pinning our hopes on posterity, in the end posterity will have lost the faintest memory of us (11).

Here we must stop to clarify two things. First, on a point of detail, what are we to make of the famous saying, *There is nothing new under the sun*? How strictly is it meant? Probably our own popular use of it gives the best answer. We exclaim it as a sweeping comment on the human scene, not as a pronouncement about inventions. No-one—least of all Qoheleth—is going to deny the inventiveness of man. But *plus ça change, plus c'est la même chose*: the more things change, the more they turn out to be the same. In their new guise the old ways go on. As a race, we never learn.

The second question is just how much is meant by the theme of the endless round. To some writers it smacks of the Stoics and their utterly circular view of time, whereby the whole web of existence must weave its selfsame pattern again and again, down to the last detail, at predetermined intervals for ever. By this token the whole future would be fated to lead round again to the very situation in which you, the reader, now find yourself; and not once but times without number.

By themselves, verses 9 and 10 (*What has been is what will be . . .*) could mean just this. But their setting is in a book which will treat moral choices as genuine by using such words as 'righteous' and 'wicked', and by pointing to a coming judgment, which would be meaningless if we were caught in a process which gave us no alternatives. What we *are* shown is the weariness of doing much and getting nowhere; and while this is very different from the fatalism we have been looking at, it is also far from the sense of pilgrimage which dominates the Old Testament.

Is this a sign of fading conviction? Gerhard von Rad reckoned that with this author 'the Wisdom literature lost its last contact with Israel's old way of thinking in terms of saving history and, quite consistently, fell back on the cyclical way of thinking common to the East, . . . only . . . in an utterly secular form'.[2] That is fair comment, if 'the cyclical way of thinking' means simply a

[2] G. von Rad, *Old Testament Theology* (Eng. Tr., Oliver and Boyd, 1962), I, p. 455.

preoccupation with the round of the seasons and the rhythms of life.[3] But it is easy to forget that if Qoheleth is taking the stance of the worldly man to show what it involves, this is the very outlook he must expound. And if he is doing so to expose it and create a hunger for something better, as the final chapters will show, he should not be identified with it except by virtue of his fellow-feeling and depth of insight.

[3] O. Loretz, *Qohelet und der Alte Orient* (Herder, 1964), pp. 247 ff., criticizes von Rad and others for describing the thought of the ancient East or of Qoheleth as cyclical. But by cyclical Loretz means the rigid determinism of the Stoic system (Loretz, p. 251), which von Rad is not discussing at this point.

Ecclesiastes 1:12—2:26
The search for satisfaction

The seeker

1:12 *I the Preacher have been king over Israel in Jerusalem.* [13] *And I applied my mind to seek and to search out by wisdom all that is done under heaven.*

The poem which we have just pondered set the tone of the book by its motto-theme and by its picture of a world endlessly busy and hopelessly inconclusive.

Now the focus sharpens. We turn from analogies and impressions to what we can know directly from experience. We are to scan a great spread of human pursuits, to ask whether anything on earth can be found which has lasting value. The author gets across to us the urgency of the search: we find ourselves involved in it. But his curious blend of titles for himself, 'Qoheleth' and 'King', alerts us to the dual character in which he is speaking, as we saw at the outset.[1] For the purpose of this passage the preacher has become a second Solomon, so that in our imagination we can do the same. Armed with such advantages, our search will be no circumscribed or tentative affair, but royal, exploring whatever the world can offer to a man of unlimited genius and wealth. In this line of country we can take his findings as definitive. To quote his words (2:12), 'What can the man do who comes after the king?'

[1] See the comments on 1:1 (p. 21). With the expression in verse 12, 'I was (or, became) king' (as it would most naturally be translated), compare Zc. 11:7 ff.: 'So I became the shepherd . . . I destroyed the three shepherds . . .', *etc.*, which likewise uses autobiographical language, not to be taken literally, or with intent to deceive, but to present to us an illuminating sequence of events with much vividness.

Perhaps, in passing, we can compare this roving reconnaissance with another passage written in the first person: the heart-searchings of Paul at the end of Romans 7. Each of these two confessions has a wider reference than to the one man who is speaking. Between them, Qoheleth and Paul explore for us man's outer and inner worlds: his search for meaning and his struggle for moral victory.

With his usual devastating candour Qoheleth is quick to tell us the worst. The search has come to nothing. To spare us the disappointment of our hopes, he warns us of the outcome (1:13b–15) before he takes us through his journey (1:16—2:11); finally he will share with us the conclusions he has reached (2:12–26).

The summary

1:13 *It is an unhappy business that God has given to the sons of men to be busy with.* 14 *I have seen everything that is done under the sun; and behold, all is vanity and a striving after wind.*

15 *What is crooked cannot be made straight,*
and what is lacking cannot be numbered.

Unobtrusively, but significantly, Qoheleth sums up his findings in terms which for a brief moment go right outside the secularist's field of vision. He sees the restlessness of life which any observer could report, but he traces it to the will of God. It is He who has *given* it to the sons of men. This may sound more like bitterness than faith, but in fact it drops a clue to something positive which will be picked up in the final chapters. At worst it would imply that there was sense, not the nonsense of chance, behind our situation, even if the sense were wholly daunting. But it can equally well chime in with the purposeful discipline which God imposed upon us as the sequel to the Fall. That was how Paul—with an evident glance at Ecclesiastes—was to interpret the travail of the world: 'for the creation was subjected to futility (or, 'vanity', AV) . . . by the will of him who subjected it *in hope.*'[2]

That hope, however, lies quite beyond our own attaining, as the ensuing search will show. And verse 15 throws in two more reminders of our limitations, with the curtness of a proverb. TEV catches it well: 'you can't straighten out what is crooked;

2 Rom. 8:20.

you can't count things that aren't there.' Whether this crookedness and this lack mean our own flaws of character or the circumstances that we can do nothing to alter,[3] we are faced again with the meagreness of what man can do. With this warning we now join Qoheleth in his series of experiments.

The sampling of life

1:16 *I said to myself, 'I have acquired great wisdom, surpassing all who were over Jerusalem before me; and my mind has had great experience of wisdom and knowledge.'* [17] *And I applied my mind to know wisdom and to know madness and folly. I perceived that this also is but a striving after wind.*

[18] *For in much wisdom is much vexation,*
    and he who increases knowledge increases sorrow.

2:1 *I said to myself, 'Come now, I will make a test of pleasure; enjoy yourself.' But behold, this also was vanity.* [2] *I said of laughter, 'It is mad,' and of pleasure, 'What use is it?'* [3] *I searched with my mind how to cheer my body with wine—my mind still guiding me with wisdom—and how to lay hold on folly, till I might see what was good for the sons of men to do under heaven during the few days of their life.* [4] *I made great works; I built houses and planted vineyards for myself;* [5] *I made myself gardens and parks, and planted in them all kinds of fruit trees.* [6] *I made myself pools from which to water the forest of growing trees.* [7] *I bought male and female slaves, and had slaves who were born in my house; I had also great possessions of herds and flocks, more than any who had been before me in Jerusalem.* [8] *I also gathered for myself silver and gold and the treasure of kings and provinces; I got singers, both men and women, and many concubines, man's delight.*

[9] *So I became great and surpassed all who were before me in Jerusalem; also my wisdom remained with me.* [10] *And whatever my eyes desired I did not keep from them; I kept my heart from no pleasure, for my heart found pleasure in all my toil, and this was my reward for all my toil.* [11] *Then I considered all that my hands had done and the toil I had spent in doing it, and behold, all was vanity and a striving after wind, and there was nothing to be gained under the sun.*

---

[3] The second alternative seems the more likely, in view of 7:13 with 7:29, which speak of God as the author of 'crooked' things, in the sense of awkward and obstinate facts, but not of moral evil.

For so famous a thinker the search must naturally begin with wisdom, the quality most highly praised in his circle. But he says nothing of its first principle, the fear of the Lord, and we can assume that the wisdom he speaks of is (as his method demands) the best thinking that man can do on his own. It is splendid, as far as it goes; nothing else can compare with it (2:13); yet it has no answer to our misgivings about life. It only sharpens them by its clarity.

So Qoheleth is taking wisdom with proper seriousness, as a discipline concerned with ultimate questions, not simply a tool for getting things done. If that were all, we should ask no more of it than wordly success. But wisdom is concerned with truth, and truth compels us to admit that success can go bad on us, and that nothing on earth has any permanence. He will have more to say on this; meanwhile his first point of rest has given way.

So he will plunge into frivolity. But part of him stands back from it all —*my mind still guiding me with wisdom*—to see what frivolity as a life-style implies, and what it does to a man. He notes at once the 'paradox of hedonism', that the more you hunt for pleasure, the less of it you find. In any case, he is looking for something beyond it and through it, for this is more than simple indulgence. It is a deliberate flight from rationality, to get at some secret of life to which reason may be blocking the way. This is the force of verse 3b (which RSV translates more faithfully than, *e.g.*, NEB or TEV): 'how to lay hold on folly, till I might see what was good for the sons of men . . .'

Here we are brought very near to our own times with their cult of the irrational in its various forms, from romanticism down to the addict's craving for strange states of consciousness; and down still further into the nihilism which cultivates the ugly, the obscene and the absurd, not as a frolic but as an attack on reasonable values. While nothing as developed as this appears in Qoheleth, his assessment of his experiment with folly shows that he is disturbed as well as disappointed. The mild disparagement of pleasure, *'What use is it?'*, is supplemented by the sharper verdict on laughter, *'It is mad'*; and in Scripture both 'madness' and 'folly' imply moral perversity rather than mental oddity.[4] To earn such a

[4] *E.g.*, in 9:3 'madness' is partnered by 'evil', and in 10:13 the present word for 'folly' is seen as a step towards 'wicked madness'. Likewise, to act foolishly (using the related verb to 'folly') usually implies a fatally headstrong attitude: *cf.* 1 Sa. 13:13; 26:21; 2 Sa. 24:10.

rebuke, the laughter that goes with this way of life must be cynical and destructive. If so, we are not far from our own black comedy and sick humour.

As if he had over-reacted in turning to the futile pleasures, he now gives himself to the joys of creativity. He bends his energies to a project worthy of his aesthetic gifts, his grasp of skills and sciences, and his ability to command a great establishment. He creates a little world within a world: multiform, harmonious, exquisite: a secular Garden of Eden, full of civilized and agreeably uncivilized delights (8),[5] with no forbidden fruits—or none that he regards as such (10). He has had the sense, for all this, to avoid the rich man's boredom by strenuous activity, enjoyed and valued for its own sake (10); and he has kept an appraising eye on his projects, even while in full pursuit of them. 'My wisdom', he tells us, 'remained with me' (9). He has not lost sight of the quest, the search for meaning, which was the mainspring of it all.

In the end, what has it yielded? A less exacting mind than Qoheleth's would have found a great deal to report with satisfaction. The achievements had been brilliant. On the material level, the farmer's perennial ambition to make (in our phrase) 'two blades of grass grow where one had grown before' had been overwhelmingly fulfilled; while aesthetically he had produced a connoisseur's paradise. If 'a thing of beauty is a joy for ever', he had not searched in vain for what is timeless and absolute.

So we tend to think.

Qoheleth will have none of it. To call such things eternal is no more than rhetoric, and nothing perishable will satisfy him. In the brutally colloquial terms of Today's English Version, his report is, 'I realized that it didn't mean a thing. It was like chasing the wind.'

The assessment

2:12 *So I turned to consider wisdom and madness and folly; for what can the man do who comes after the king? Only what he has already done.*

[5] The word *šiddâ*, occurring only here, is taken to mean 'musical instrument' in AV. But in a letter from Pharaoh Amenophis III to Milkilu prince of Gezer (translation in *ANET*, p. 487a), demanding 40 concubines, the Egyptian word for concubine is accompanied by an explanatory Canaanite word akin to *šiddâ*. Although NEB prefers to make no conjecture, and JB offers the word 'chests' (*i.e.*, treasure-chests), RSV seems likely to be right with 'concubines', as in RV (*cf.* TEV, 'women').

¹³ *Then I saw that wisdom excels folly as light excels darkness.* ¹⁴ *The wise man has his eyes in his head, but the fool walks in darkness; and yet I perceived that one fate comes to all of them.* ¹⁵ *Then I said to myself, 'What befalls the fool will befall me also; why then have I been so very wise?' And I said to myself that this also is vanity.* ¹⁶ *For of the wise man as of the fool there is no enduring remembrance, seeing that in the days to come all will have been long forgotten. How the wise man dies just like the fool!* ¹⁷ *So I hated life, because what is done under the sun was grievous to me; for all is vanity and a striving after wind.*

18 *I hated all my toil in which I had toiled under the sun, seeing that I must leave it to the man who will come after me;* ¹⁹ *and who knows whether he will be a wise man or a fool? Yet he will be master of all for which I toiled and used my wisdom under the sun. This also is vanity.* ²⁰ *So I turned about and gave my heart up to despair over all the toil of my labours under the sun,* ²¹ *because sometimes a man who has toiled with wisdom and knowledge and skill must leave all to be enjoyed by a man who did not toil for it. This also is vanity and a great evil.* ²² *What has a man from all the toil and strain with which he toils beneath the sun?* ²³ *For all his days are full of pain, and his work is a vexation; even in the night his mind does not rest. This also is vanity.*

24 *There is nothing better for a man than that he should eat and drink, and find enjoyment in his toil. This also, I saw, is from the hand of God;* ²⁵ *for apart from him who can eat or who can have enjoyment?* ²⁶ *For to the man who pleases him God gives wisdom and knowledge and joy; but to the sinner he gives the work of gathering and heaping, only to give to one who pleases God. This also is vanity and a striving after wind.*

The brief and blunt verdict of verse 11 needed some spelling out, for in delving into life's possibilities Qoheleth was not acting purely on his own account. If he of all people has come back empty-handed, even in the mantle of Solomon, what hope has anyone else (12)?⁶ So he goes back to the great alternatives, wisdom and folly, to compare them and then to assess them radically. Has either of them an answer to this search for something final? They were the two ways of life he had been testing in the experiments of 1:17—2:10—for he includes in 'folly' not only

---

⁶ TEV tampers with the meaning of verse 12 by reversing the order of its two main clauses and translating 12b (its own 12a) as '. . . a king can only do what previous kings have done'—which is manifestly untrue. NEB resorts to a different transposition, removing 12b to the end of verse 18.

33

the 'madness' of self-indulgence and cynicism but the pursuit of pleasure at any level, even the highest, as an escape from painful thoughts that should be faced. This was clear enough from the sequel to 1:18, where it was the comment, 'he who increases knowledge increases sorrow', which led to the brisk resolve, 'Come now, I will make a test of pleasure; enjoy yourself.'

The bare comparison of wisdom and folly is simple, but the final assessment is shattering. Nothing could be more obvious than that the two compare with one another as light with darkness (13, 14a); but Qoheleth has the wit to remember that they are abstractions and we are men. It is little use commending to us the ultimate worth of wisdom, if in the end none of us will be around to exercise it, let alone to value it. This of course is why the purely human achievements which we call lasting are nothing of the kind. As men of the world we may revere them in this way, but only for lack of Qoheleth's honesty in seeing that *in the days to come all will have been long forgotten* (16). He has no illusions, though by rights it is we who should have none—we who have heard from the secularists themselves that our very planet is dying.

So, for the first time in the book but by no means the last, the fact of death brings the search to a sudden stop. If *one fate comes to all*, and that fate is extinction, it robs every man of his dignity and every project of its point. We look at these two results in turn in verses 14–17 and 18–23.

As to man's dignity, what is so mortifying (an appropriate word!) about death's final levelling of wise men and fools—to which we could add, 'good men and bad', 'saints and sadists', and every other pair of opposites—is that if it is true, it allows the last word to a brute fact which tramples on every value-judgment we can make. Everything may tell us that wisdom is *not* on a par with folly, nor goodness with evil; but no matter: if death is the end of the road, the contention that there is nothing to choose between them will get the last word. The choices that we positively knew to be significant will be brushed aside as finally irrelevant.

So I hated life. If there is a lie at the centre of existence, and non-sense at the end of it, who has the heart to make anything of it? If, as we might put it, every card in our hand will be trumped, does it matter how we play? Why treat a king with more respect than a knave?

Incidentally, this bitter reaction is a witness to our ability to stand clear of our condition and to weigh it up. To be outraged at what is universal and unavoidable suggests something of a divine discontent, a hint of what the great saying in 3:11 will call 'eternity' in man's mind. In fact our verse 16 uses that word to lament the lack of any *enduring* remembrance of the wise.

Verses 18–23 look at a smaller grief, but one which can sap the spirit in its own way: the frustrating uncertainty of all our enterprises once they slip from our control, as sooner or later they must. On his own principles, the man of the world should hardly object to this, provided they last his time; yet he does mind, for he shares our inbuilt longing for what is permanent. The more he has toiled at his life's work (and verses 22 f. show how obsessive this toil can be), the more galling will be the thought of its fruits falling into other hands—and as likely as not, the wrong hands. This is yet another blow to the hope, glimpsed earlier in the chapter, of finding fulfilment in hard work and high attainment. Their very success will accentuate the anticlimax.

At last a more cheerful note breaks in. Perhaps we have been trying too hard. The compulsive worker of verses 22 f., overloading his days with toil and his nights with worry, has missed the simple joys that God was holding out to him. The real issue for him was not between work and rest but, had he known it, between meaningless and meaningful activity. As verse 24 points out, the very toil that tyrannized him was potentially a joyful gift of God (and joy itself is another, 25),[7] if only he had had the grace to take it as such.

Here is the other side to the 'unhappy business that God has given to the sons of men' (1:13), for in themselves, and rightly used, the basic things of life are sweet and good. Food, drink and work are samples of them, and Qoheleth will remind us of others.[8] What spoils them is our hunger to get out of them more than they can give; a symptom of the longing which differentiates us from the beasts, but whose misdirection is the underlying theme of this book.

So, for a moment, the veil is lifted in verse 26, to show us

[7] The words, *apart from him* (25) are an emendation, supported by LXX. The MT has 'apart from me', which would make good sense only if God were speaking in the first person. AV, RV, 'more than I', is intelligible, but scarcely a possible translation.

[8] *Cf.* 9:7–10; 11:7–10.

something other than futility. The book will end strongly on this positive note, but meanwhile we are shown enough in such glimpses to assure us that there is an answer, and that the author is no defeatist. He disillusions us to bring us to reality.

What he is saying in this final verse could be carelessly read as an escape-clause for God's favourites, sparing them the material risks which have just been described. Today's English Version goes out of its way to give this impression by removing the word 'sinner' (for no reason) and by describing those who please God merely as 'those he likes' or 'likes better' than others. But even without that gratuitous distortion it would be easy to overlook the vital contrast in this verse, which is between the satisfying spiritual gifts of God (wisdom, knowledge, joy), which only those who please Him can desire or receive, and the frustrating business [9] of amassing what cannot be kept, a business which is the chosen lot of those who reject Him. The fact that in the end the sinner's hoard will go to the righteous is only a crowning irony to what was in any case *vanity and a striving after wind*. And for the righteous it is a crowning vindication, but no more. Like the meek, who are promised the earth, their treasure is elsewhere and of another kind.

[9] *Work*, in this verse, is the same word as 'business' in the phrase of 1:13, 'it is an unhappy business that God has given to the sons of men to be busy with'. TEV creates a further misleading contrast, namely between those to whom God gives His gifts and those who have to work for what they get.

Ecclesiastes 3:1–15
The tyranny of time

3:1 For everything there is a season, and a time for every matter under heaven:

² a time to be born, and a time to die;
 a time to plant, and a time to pluck up what is planted;
³ a time to kill, and a time to heal;
 a time to break down, and a time to build up;
⁴ a time to weep, and a time to laugh;
 a time to mourn, and a time to dance;
⁵ a time to cast away stones, and a time to gather stones together;
 a time to embrace, and a time to refrain from embracing;
⁶ a time to seek, and a time to lose;
 a time to keep, and a time to cast away;
⁷ a time to rend, and a time to sew;
 a time to keep silence, and a time to speak;
⁸ a time to love, and a time to hate;
 a time for war, and a time for peace.
⁹ What gain has the worker from his toil?

10 I have seen the business that God has given to the sons of men to be busy with. ¹¹ He has made everything beautiful in its time; also he has put eternity into man's mind, yet so that he cannot find out what God has done from the beginning to the end. ¹² I know that there is nothing better for them than to be happy and enjoy themselves as long as they live; ¹³ also that it is God's gift to man that every one should eat and drink and take pleasure in all his toil. ¹⁴ I know that whatever God does endures for ever; nothing can be added to it, nor anything taken from it; God has made it so, in order that men should fear before him. ¹⁵ That which is, already has been; that which is to be, already has been; and God seeks what has been driven away.

Perhaps 'tyranny' is too strong a word for the gentle ebb and flow described here, which carries us all our days from one kind of activity to its opposite, and back again. The description is pleasing, with its varieties of mood and action and its hints of different rhythms in our affairs. Rhythm itself appeals to us, for who would wish for perpetual spring—'a time to plant' but never to pick—or envy the sleepless businessman who met us in the last chapter?

Yet in the context of a quest for finality, not only is a movement to and fro no better than the endless circling of chapter one, but it has disturbing implications of its own. One of them is that we dance to a tune, or many tunes, not of our own making; a second is that nothing we pursue has any permanence. We throw ourselves into some absorbing activity which offers us fulfilment, but how freely did we choose it? How soon shall we be doing the exact opposite? Perhaps our choices are no freer than our responses to winter and summer, childhood and old age, dictated by the march of time and of unbidden change.

Looked at in this way, the repetition of 'a time . . ., and a time . . .' begins to be oppressive. Whatever may be our skill and initiative, our real masters seem to be these inexorable seasons: not only those of the calendar, but that tide of events which moves us now to one kind of action which seems fitting, now to another which puts it all into reverse. Obviously we have little say in the situations which move us to *weep* or *laugh*, *mourn* or *dance*; but our more deliberate acts, too, may be time-conditioned more than we suppose. 'Who would have imagined', we sometimes say, 'that the day would come when I should find myself doing such-and-such, and seeing it as my duty!' So the peace-loving nation prepares for war; or the shepherd takes the knife to the creature he has earlier nursed back to health. The collector disperses his hoard; friends part in bitter conflict; the need to speak out follows the need to be silent. Nothing that we do, it seems, is free from this relativity and this pressure—almost dictation—from outside.

Our natural reaction might be to seek reality in something beyond the reach of change, treating the world of everyday experience as a mere distraction. Surprisingly, and superbly, Qoheleth in verse 11 enables us to see perpetual change not as something unsettling but as an unfolding pattern, scintillating and God-given. The trouble for us is not that life refuses to keep still, but that we see only a fraction of its movement and of its subtle, intricate design. Instead of changelessness, there is something better: a dynamic, divine purpose, with its *beginning* and *end*. Instead of frozen perfection there is the kaleidoscopic movement of innumerable processes, each with its own character and its period of blossoming and ripening, *beautiful in its time* and contributing to the over-all masterpiece which is the work of one Creator. We catch these brilliant moments, but even apart from the darkness interspersed with them they leave us unsatisfied for lack of any total meaning that we can grasp. Unlike the animals, immersed in time, we long to see them in their full context, for we know something of eternity: enough at least to compare the fleeting with the 'for ever'.[1] We are like the desperately near-sighted, inching their way along some great tapestry or fresco in the attempt to take it in. We see enough to recognize something of its quality, but the grand design escapes us, for we can never stand back far enough to view it as its Creator does, whole and entire, *from the beginning to the end*.

This incomprehensibility is dismaying for the thoughtful secularist, but not for the believer. Both can take refuge in making the most of life as it is, but the man of no faith is doing it in the void. Verse 12 is not as frivolous as may appear from RSV, where *enjoy themselves* is literally 'do good', *i.e.*, 'do the best he can' (TEV; *cf*. NEB); yet even so, the final phrase, *as long as they live*, casts a shadow over every enterprise. If nothing is permanent, even though much of our work may long survive us, we are only filling in time; and the chill of that thought will seep into us sooner or later.

The believer, on the other hand, can accept the same kind of unpretentious programme, not as a stopgap but as an assignment. It is a *gift* from God (13), an allotted portion in life, whose purpose is known to the Giver and is part of His everlasting work; for God does nothing in vain. As verse 14 points out, His plans unlike ours need no corrections or amendments: they endure. The *for ever* of this verse matches the *eternity* put *into man's mind*

[1] *Eternity* (11) is the same word as 'ever' in 14, but used here as a noun. LXX translates it here and elsewhere by *aiōn*, the noun which yields the NT adjective 'eternal'. Although it can be used merely for time past or future (*cf*. NEB and, very loosely, TEV), or for an age, the contrast to the word *time* (*i.e.*, season) in 11a points to a strong rather than a weak sense for it in this verse. AV, RV have 'the world' here, used in the archaic sense of an age (*cf*. the phrase 'world without end').

(11). To have some share in this, however modest, is to escape the 'vanity of vanities'.

So the whole paragraph speaks with the simultaneous 'kindness and severity' which meet us in the well-known phrase of Romans 11:22, expounded there as 'severity towards those who have fallen, but God's kindness to you . . .'. The earthbound man, in the light of our verses 14 and 15, and of this whole section, is the prisoner of a system he cannot break or even bend; and behind it is God. There is no escape, and nowhere to jettison what encumbers or incriminates him. But the man of God hears these verses with no such misgivings. To him verse 14 describes the divine faithfulness which makes the *fear* of God a fruitful, filial relationship;[2] and verse 15 assures him that with God all is foreknown, and nothing overlooked.[3] God has no abortive enterprises or forgotten men. Once again Qoheleth has shown, in passing, that the despair he describes is not his own, and need not be ours.

But he has more facts about the world to point out. He turns now to the scene of human society, and the way we exercise power.

[2] *Cf.* Ps. 130:4, where it rests on the divine forgiveness.

[3] *What has been driven away* I take to mean 'what is past'; *cf.* AV. God's 'seeking' of it will be either to judge or to retrieve, depending on the nature of what is sought. Other interpretations have seen *driven away* as a synonym for the persecuted, which is quite often the case but hardly seems appropriate here; or the whole phrase as an expression of God's relentless chasing of events into the past, and round again into the future.

Ecclesiastes 3:16—4:3
The harshness of life

3:16 *Moreover I saw under the sun that in the place of justice, even there was wickedness, and in the place of righteousness, even there was wickedness.* [17] *I said in my heart, God will judge the righteous and the wicked, for he has appointed a time for every matter, and for every work.* [18] *I said in my heart with regard to the sons of men that God is testing them to show them that they are but beasts.* [19] *For the fate of the sons of men and the fate of beasts is the same; as one dies, so dies the other. They all have the same breath, and man has no advantage over the beasts; for all is vanity.* [20] *All go to one place; all are from the dust, and all turn to dust again.* [21] *Who knows whether the spirit of man goes upward and the spirit of the beast goes down to the earth?* [22] *So I saw that there is nothing better than that a man should enjoy his work, for that is his lot; who can bring him to see what will be after him?*

4:1 *Again I saw all the oppressions that are practised under the sun. And behold, the tears of the oppressed, and they had no one to comfort them! On the side of their oppressors there was power, and there was no one to comfort them.* [2] *And I thought the dead who are already dead more fortunate than the living who are still alive;* [3] *but better than both is he who has not yet been, and has not seen the evil deeds that are done under the sun.*

This is not altogether a change of subject, for the thought of set times and their power over us is still present in verse 17. But the problem of injustice is too poignant to be left as a mere illustration of that theme. It becomes an issue on its own for a short while in chapter 4, and will return at intervals in later passages.[1]

First, though, it is seen in the setting of life's reversals and sud-

---

[1] See 5:8 f.; 8:10–15; 9:13–16; 10:5–7; 10:16 f.

den shifts, which are the dominant interest of chapter 3. For if anything cries out to be reversed it is injustice. Here at last is some obvious gain from the twists and turns of our affairs. The fact that everything on earth is seasonal promises an end to the long winter of evil and misrule. It reinforces the purely moral conviction that *God will judge* (17), by the realization that for this event, as for everything else, He has already appointed its proper time.

This is all very well, we may feel; but why the delay? Why is the present not the proper time for universal justice? To that unspoken question verses 18 ff. give a typically abrasive answer, since our first need is not to teach God His business but to learn the truth about ourselves, a lesson we are very slow to accept. (Even the twentieth century finds us still inclined to deny our inborn sinfulness.) So when verse 18 says, *God is testing* (or better, exposing)[2] *them to show them that they are but beasts*, it shocks us deeply. True, RSV's '*but* beasts' is questionable.[3] But we have to admit that quite apart from our tendencies to cruelty and squalor, which put us in a class even below the beasts, there are at least two facts about us which support the charge: the role of greed and cunning in our affairs (which is the subject under discussion, verse 16), and the mortality which man shares with all earthly creatures. The first of these sad facts reappears in the next chapter; the second occupies the remainder of this one, and interacts with other parts of the Old Testament. Verse 20, showing us man on his journey from dust to dust, as in Genesis 3:19, confronts us with the Fall, and with the irony that we die like cattle because we fancied ourselves as gods.

But does something within us survive death? From its chosen

[2] The word for 'testing' already seems to have its later sense of 'bringing to light' (*cf.* McNeile, p. 64). So AV, 'that God might manifest them'.

[3] The text need be saying no more than that men are beasts to each other, or are beasts in certain respects indicated by the context. This rather difficult verse runs: '. . . for God to test (or expose—see previous footnote) them, and to see that they are beasts, they for them(selves)'. On 'see', *cf.* perhaps the vividness of Ps. 14:2; otherwise the implied subject may be the people involved ('that they may see', RV, *cf.* AV); but a change of vowel gives 'show' (RSV and most moderns, following LXX *et al.*). The words 'they for them(selves)' have been interpreted as part of a copying error (*cf.*, diversely, NEB, TEV) since 'beast' and 'they' are similar words; or as meaning 'to each other' ('and expose them for the brute beasts they are to each other', JB); or as 'they for their part'; or as 'they in and of themselves' (Delitzsch). I incline to Delitzsch or to JB.

standpoint, Ecclesiastes can only reply, *Who knows?* [4] *Breath*, or *spirit*, [5] in these verses is the life God gives to animals and men alike, whose withdrawal means their death, as Psalm 104:29 f. points out. Clearly we have at least that much in common with the beasts; but whether 'spirit' implies anything eternal for us, no-one can decide by observation. [6]

Yet the echo of Psalm 49, which makes the same comparison between men and beasts, reminds us that there *is* an answer. There the man of faith can say, 'But God will ransom my soul from the power of Sheol, for he will receive me.' It is 'man in his pomp', man without understanding, who is 'like the beasts that perish'; [7] and this is the man with whom Ecclesiastes is concerned.

To such a person verse 22 offers the best it can: the temporary satisfaction of doing a job well. It is not to be despised. The possibility of it is a legacy from a world well created, as verse 13 made clear. All that will be missing—but it is virtually everything—is the fulfilment to be found in accepting such work as the Creator's gift (see above, on verse 13), and offering it up to Him.

With chapter 4:1-3 we return to *the oppressions that are practised under the sun*, the subject broached in 3:16. The passage is as brief as it is painful, for if there is no way of ending these things (as indeed there is none in this present age) there is little to add to the bitter facts of verse 1 beyond the lament of verses 2 and 3. We may think this attitude defeatist, for there is always much that can be done for sufferers, given the will to do it. Yet this objection would hardly be fair. Qoheleth is surveying the scene as a whole, and he might well retort that after every conceivable intervention there would still remain innumerable pockets of oppression in

[4] AV stands virtually alone, against all the ancient versions and now the modern ones, in translating verse 21 as an implied affirmation: 'Who knoweth the spirit of man that goeth upward', *etc.* The Heb. vowel at the beginning of 'goeth' favours AV (though not exclusively: see Heb. of, *e.g.*, Nu. 16:22; Lv. 10:19), but the *hî'* which follows it tells against this. The standpoint generally maintained by Qoheleth, and the present context in particular, support the translation, 'Who knows whether . . .?'

[5] Both are translations of *rûaḥ* here (19, 21). A different word is used in Gn. 2:7 for the breath of life breathed into man's nostrils at his creation.

[6] At first sight, Ec. 12:7 answers this question. But it need not be saying more than is said in Ps. 104:29 f., that God gives and withdraws His creatures' life-breath at will.

[7] Ps. 49:12, 14, 15, 20. RSV robs the psalm of its climax by making verse 20 merely repeat verse 12, whereas in the Heb. text it clarifies it with the phrase, '(man) who does not understand'.

'the habitations of cruelty';[8] enough to make angels weep, if not men. He could add that there is no coincidence in the fact that power is found on the side of the oppressor, since it is power that most quickly breeds the habit of oppression. Paradoxically it limits the possibility of reform itself, because the more control the reformer wields, the more it tends to tyranny.

So another aspect of earthly life has been exposed; and there is nothing sadder in the whole book than the wistful glance in verses 2 and 3 at the dead and the unborn, who are spared the sight of so much anguish. This is fitting, for in general Ecclesiastes is concerned with frustration, but here with the reign of evil, and evil in its hideous form of cruelty. If Qoheleth's gloom strikes us as excessive at this point, we may need to ask whether our more cheerful outlook springs from hope and not complacency. While we, as Christians, see further ahead than he allowed himself to look, it is no reason to spare ourselves the realities of the present.

[8] *Cf.* Ps. 74:20, AV.

Ecclesiastes 4:4–8
The rat-race

4:4 *Then I saw that all toil and all skill in work come from a man's envy of his neighbour. This also is vanity and a striving after wind.*

5 The fool folds his hands, and eats his own flesh.

6 Better is a handful of quietness than two hands full of toil and a striving after wind.

7 Again, I saw vanity under the sun: [8] *a person who has no one, either son or brother, yet there is no end to all his toil, and his eyes are never satisfied with riches, so that he never asks, 'For whom am I toiling and depriving myself of pleasure?' This also is vanity and an unhappy business.*

In this little sample of attitudes to work we are reminded of some strange but familiar extremes. First, the competitive urge. Verse 4 must not be pressed too hard, for this writer like any other must be free to make his points vigorously. We may quibble if we will, and remind him of such people as solitary castaways or needy peasants, who toil simply to keep alive, or those artists who really love perfection for its own sake; but the fact remains that all too much of our hard work and high endeavour is mixed with the craving to outshine or not to be outshone. Even in friendly rivalry this may play a larger part than we think—for we can bear to be outclassed for some of the time and by some people, but not too regularly or too profoundly. To feel oneself a failure is to discover in one's soul the envy that Qoheleth detects here, in its pathetic form of resentments nursed and grievances enjoyed.[1]

[1] McNeile points out that the Heb. of this verse simply makes envy the predicate of toil and skill. *I.e.*, "'I saw . . . that *it meant* the jealousy *etc.*"—it was both incited by it and resulted in it.' Most modern translations take envy

The second little portrait (verse 5) shows the contrary extreme: the drop-out. He disdains these frantic rivalries. But he is given his real name, *the fool*, for his inertia is an equal and opposite error to theirs. He is the picture of complacency and unwitting self-destruction, for this comment on him points out a deeper damage than the wasting of his capital. His idleness eats away not only what he has but what he is: eroding his self-control, his grasp of reality, his capacity for care and, in the end, his self-respect.

To both these unhappy ways of life verse 6 holds out the true alternative. The beautiful expression, *a handful of quietness*, manages to convey the twofold thought of modest demands and inward peace: an attitude as far removed from the fool's selfish indolence as from the thruster's scramble for pre-eminence.

> 'Give me my scallop-shell of quiet,
>   My staff of faith to walk upon,
> My scrip of joy, immortal diet,
>   My bottle of salvation,
> My gown of glory, hope's true gage,
> And thus I'll take my pilgrimage.'[2]

But if anything can be more tyrannous than envy, that thing is habit, when habit has turned into fixation. Verses 7 and 8 picture the compulsive money-maker as someone virtually dehumanized, for he has surrendered to a mere craving and to the endless process of feeding it. Suddenly the writer identifies himself with this man, and enables us to do the same, by voicing for him the question, *'For whom am I toiling . . .?'*—for these words come unannounced,[3] as though to articulate what the man's whole life is saying. Although it is for the sake of clarity that we are looking at a man with no family, we may well feel that his loneliness is no accident and that he will have no friends either, living for his routine as he does. Such a man, even with a wife and children, will have little time for them, convinced that he is toiling for their

---

as the incitement to success; AV, RV take it to be the effect of achievement on others; the Heb. leaves both possibilities open.

[2] Sir Walter Raleigh, 'His Pilgrimage'.

[3] RSV has added the words, *so that he never asks*. This assumes too much, as does AV. It is more accurate simply to insert, 'he asks' (NEB, *cf*. RV); better still, to leave the question unintroduced (JB).

benefit although his heart is elsewhere, devoted and wedded to his projects.

This picture of lonely, pointless busyness, equally with that of jealous rivalry in verse 4, checks any excessive claims we might wish to make for the blessings of hard work. Not with this—though still less with the idleness of verse 8—lies the answer to frustration.

At this point Qoheleth seems to pause in his search for what is lasting in life, and we can seize our chance of looking back over the stretch of country we have covered with him up to now.

A first summary
A backward glance over
Ecclesiastes 1:1—4:8

So far, in our survey of the earthly scene, we have looked at what the world can offer at four or five different levels. We began with an impression of its utter restlessness, the endless, inconclusive repetitions to be found in nature and in the human scene (1:1-11). Then we sampled the satisfactions of different life-styles, rational and irrational, frivolous and austere: the pleasures of art and toil, of the moment and of building for the future (1:12—2:26). If some of these had much to give, none survived the acid test of death. To find anything that time would not undo, we should have to look elsewhere. But time, as it displayed itself in chapter 3, not only 'bears all its sons away' but meanwhile floats us back and forth by tides and currents that are too strong for us. We are not the masters of our situation: we cannot even get our bearings in it.

A more sinister note crept in at 3:16 with the theme of human tyranny and cruelty, that bitter fact that can make death, even at its most hopeless, seem no longer the last enemy, as it met us in chapter 2, but the last remaining friend.

Finally we contemplated in 4:4-8 not the losers in this human struggle but the apparent winners and survivors: those who manage to be utterly absorbed in it or in themselves. To all appearance they have come to terms with life; but have they won a prize that they can keep?—and does their way of winning it bear inspection? Our modern term, the rat-race, sums up the burden of these verses: a frantic rivalry at one extreme, a disastrous opting-out at the other; and for the successful few, a life devoted to acquiring prize after pointless prize.

After this unsparing assessment it will be a relief to turn for a while from our desperate search for something ultimate, to matters close at hand—for life goes on while we are searching, and there are better and worse ways of living it. We can be wise at this level at least!

For a start, we can be more sensible than the lonely, obsessive moneymaker we were last considering; and a wiser pattern than his will be the first subject of the comments on life that follow.

Ecclesiastes 4:9—5:12

Interlude: Some reflections, maxims and home truths

Companionship

4:9 *Two are better than one, because they have a good reward for their toil.* 10 *For if they fall, one will lift up his fellow; but woe to him who is alone when he falls and has not another to lift him up.* 11 *Again, if two lie together, they are warm; but how can one be warm alone?* 12 *And though a man might prevail against one who is alone, two will withstand him. A threefold cord is not quickly broken.*

Having looked at the poverty of the 'loner', whatever his outward success, we now reflect on something better; and *better* will be a key word here (4:9, 13; 5:1, 5), as it very often is in the value-judgments of the Wisdom writers.[1]

The thoughts are simple and direct; they apply to many forms of partnership, not least (though not explicitly) to marriage. With graceful brevity they depict the profit, resilience, comfort[2] and strength bestowed by a true alliance; and these are worth setting against the demands it may make of us. Such demands are not explicit here, but there would hardly be the need to set out the benefits of partnership if it involved no cost. Its obvious price is a person's independence: henceforth he must consult another's interest and convenience, listen to another's reasoning, adjust to another's pace and style, keep faith with another's trust. As for

[1] TEV restricts its meaning to 'better off' or 'well off' in 4:9, 13, which hardly does justice to 4:13 and breaks the link between these two sayings and the 'better' in 5:1, 5.

[2] Verse 11 could apply to marriage, but primarily perhaps to travellers, sleeping in the open. Barton observes that 'the nights of Palestine are cold . . ., and a lone traveller sleeps sometimes close to his donkey for warmth in lieu of other companionship'.

the rewards that we find here, they are all joint benefits: there is no question of one partner exploiting the other.

The *threefold cord* can be a reminder that true partnership has more than one form. While numbers, wrongly related, can be divisive or disastrous (see on verse 11), in their right form they can not only add to the benefits of union but multiply them. An obvious example of this enrichment, and a favourite among preachers, is the strength brought to a marriage, or indeed any human alliance, when God as its chief strand makes it a threefold bond. But perhaps it would be nearer to the writer's thought to read this metaphor in purely human terms, so that if it were applied to marriage the third strand would appropriately be the gift of children, with all that this adds to the quality and strength of the original tie. Even so, we are probably being more specific than he intends.

Popular acclaim

4:13 *Better is a poor and wise youth than an old and foolish king, who will no longer take advice,* **14** *even though he had gone from prison to the throne or in his own kingdom had been born poor.* **15** *I saw all the living who move about under the sun, as well as that youth, who was to stand in his place;* **16** *there was no end of all the people; he was over all of them. Yet those who come later will not rejoice in him. Surely this also is vanity and a striving after wind.*

This paragraph has its obscurities, but it portrays something familiar enough in public life: the short-lived popularity of the great. It shows the faults on both sides, beginning with the stubbornness of the man who has been too long in the saddle— who is out of touch and out of sympathy with the times, forgetting what it was like to be young, and fiery, and hard-up, as he once was himself.[3] There is enough likeness to the earlier and later David for us to reflect that the finest of men can go this way and be the last to realize it. But the portrait is not designed to be historical.

So it may come to it that a better man supplants him—and he is

[3] Opinions differ as to whether the one who has known prison and poverty (14) is the *old king* (as I would think) or the *poor and wise youth* who supplants him. If it is the latter, then verse 15 may see him ousted in his turn, since *that youth* (RSV) is lit. 'the second youth'; though it may also be translated 'the youth, the other man', *i.e.*, the old king's youthful rival.

better if he has the right qualities, whatever his lack of years or standing, as verse 13a points out. Qoheleth, with his way of bringing a scene vividly before us, pictures the teeming mass of men, and sees them on the side of [4] the newcomer, young as he is, and innumerable as they are.

Yet he too will go the way of the old king, not necessarily for his faults, but simply as time and familiarity, and the restlessness of men, make him no longer interesting. He has reached a pinnacle of human glory, only to be stranded there. It is yet another of our human anticlimaxes and ultimately empty achievements.

Pious talk

5:1 *Guard your steps when you go to the house of God; to draw near to listen is better than to offer the sacrifice of fools; for they do not know that they are doing evil.* 2 *Be not rash with your mouth, nor let your heart be hasty to utter a word before God, for God is in heaven, and you upon earth; therefore let your words be few.*

3 *For a dream comes with much business, and a fool's voice with many words.*

4 *When you vow a vow to God, do not delay paying it; for he has no pleasure in fools. Pay what you vow.* 5 *It is better that you should not vow than that you should vow and not pay.* 6 *Let not your mouth lead you into sin, and do not say before the messenger that it was a mistake; why should God be angry at your voice, and destroy the work of your hands?*

7 *For when dreams increase, empty words grow many: but do you fear God.*

Continuing with his interlude of pen-portraits, Qoheleth turns his observant eye on man as worshipper. Like the prophets, he presses for reality in this realm; but his tone is quiet, though his words are razor-sharp. Whereas the prophets hurl their invective against the vicious and the hypocrites, this writer's target is the well-meaning person who likes a good sing and turns up cheerfully enough to church; but who listens with half an ear, and never quite gets round to what he has volunteered to do for God.

[4] The expression *as well as that youth* (RSV) is lit. 'with that youth'. 'With' can mean either 'as well as' or 'joined with'. The latter prepares us better for the pre-eminence the youth enjoys in the next verse. (TEV adds interest to the RSV sense by the paraphrase, 'I realized that somewhere among them there is a young man who . . .' But this stretches it rather far.)

Such a man has forgotten where and who he is; above all, who God is. The reiterated word *fool(s)* is scathing, for to be casual with God is an *evil* (1), a *sin* (6) and a provocation which will not go unpunished (6b). If we are tempted to write this off as a piece of Old Testament harshness, the New Testament will disconcert us equally with its warnings against making pious words meaningless, or treating lightly what is holy (Mt. 7:21 ff.; 23:16 ff.; 1 Cor. 11:27 ff.). No amount of emphasis on grace can justify taking liberties with God, for the very concept of grace demands gratitude; and gratitude cannot be casual.

Going back over these verses in more detail, we are reminded by the opening words (the equivalent of our phrase, 'Watch your step!') of the pains God took to guard His earthly threshold in early times, even by the threat of death ('lest they die in their uncleanness by defiling my tabernacle', Lv. 15:31). At one level this makes clear to us both the cost of our admission to 'the heavenly sanctuary', and the purity that is demanded of us ('sprinkled clean . . ., washed with pure water': see Heb. 10:19 ff.), while at another level it brings home to us the regard we should have for the church of God, the living temple.[5]

To listen (1b) has the double force in Hebrew which it sometimes has in English: to pay attention and to obey. So this saying is close to the famous words of Samuel, 'to obey (lit. to listen) is better than sacrifice' (1 Sa. 15:22). Here, however, the meaningless worship is unwitting; one's sin is that of a fool[6] rather than a rogue, if that is any consolation! Qoheleth would hardly encourage us to think so: his reminder that God *has no pleasure in fools* (4) is as quietly crushing a remark as any in the book.

Two proverbs drive home the point by linking the chatter of fools to the unreality of dreams. The link is a little elusive in verse 3, but less so in verse 7 where the dreams appear to be daydreams, reducing worship to verbal doodling. Verse 3 seems to mean that, by its very quantity, an excess of talk is bound to throw up folly, just as an excess of business ends in troubled dreams.[7] Such a saying confronts us with the fact that fools are not a fixed

[5] *Cf.* 1 Cor. 3:16 f.; Eph. 2:19 ff.; 1 Pet. 2:5.

[6] *The sacrifice of fools* gives the right sense, but the phrase is more exactly 'than that fools should give a sacrifice' (McNeile).

[7] A suggested alternative sense is that a dream consists of ('comes in the form of') *much business* (*i.e.*, a flood of events and images), and a fool's voice consists of a flood of words. Barton inclines to this suggestion of T. Tyler, but it is doubtful whether *business* can have this meaning.

type, but people behaving in a certain way. In the context of worship, that way is to pour out a stream of pious phrases which trifle with our Sovereign (2) and outrun our actual thinking and intending. Our excuses, when eventually we are taken up on what we have said in church, will sound as lame as any hoaxer's or defaulter's.[8]

Official predators

5:8 *If you see in a province the poor oppressed and justice and right violently taken away, do not be amazed at the matter; for the high official is watched by a higher, and there are yet higher ones over them.* [9] *But in all, a king is an advantage to a land with cultivated fields.*

So the reflections on coping realistically with life continue, with Qoheleth now turning an appraising eye on bureaucracy. If the picture does not claim to be universal, still it is familiar enough. The glimpse of that vista of officials suggests possibilities of Kafka-esque evasiveness, to baffle the citizen who presses for his rights: he can be endlessly obstructed and deflected. As for moral responsibility, it can be side-stepped with equal facility. Every officer can blame the system, while the ultimate authorities hold sway at an infinite distance from the lives they affect. But Qoheleth points out another feature of bureaucracy: its predatory self-absorption, each official keeping a baleful eye on the next one down the list.[9] Delitzsch sums up the operation of this in the old Persian empire: 'The satrap stood at the head of state officers. In many cases he fleeced the province to fatten himself. But over the satrap stood inspectors, who often enough built up their own

[8] The *messenger* of verse 6 has been variously interpreted: as 'the angel' (AV, RV, JB, NEB; for the Heb. language does not distinguish between earthly and heavenly messengers); as the priest (TEV; *cf.* Mal. 2:7); as a temple official sent to collect debts and dues; and as God Himself (*cf.* the expression 'the angel of the Lord', used in this sense). Whichever of these is meant, the point at issue is the sin which his arrival exposes.

[9] AV (*cf.* RV) makes the beginning of 8b sound reassuring ('he that is higher than the highest regardeth'), but RSV is nearer to the literal Hebrew, which could be rendered, 'For high-up above high-up keeps watch, and high-ups over them'. The plural, 'high-ups', could be a plural of majesty and refer to the king or to God (*cf.* NEB); but if so, it might have been expressed more clearly (a different word is used elsewhere for God's title, the Most High). As for the verb, while 'keep watch' usually implies protection, it can also be hostile: *e.g.*, 1 Sa. 19:11.

fortunes by fatal denunciations; and over all stood the king, or rather the court, with its rivalry of intrigues among courtiers and royal women.'[1] Small wonder if the citizen at the bottom of such an edifice found justice a luxury he could not afford.

True to the standpoint of the book, the comment on all this is dry and realistic. After all, if we are looking at the world on its own terms of thoroughgoing secularism, we cannot expect too high a moral tone, either from the system we find in force or from any other. For all his hatred of injustice, Qoheleth pins no hopes on utopian schemes or on revolution. He knows what is in man.

So the first comment is, *Do not be amazed at the matter*, and the final one is, in effect, that even tyranny is better than anarchy. The point of verse 9[2] seems to be that nothing would be gained by returning to the simple structure of the old nomadic days. A developed country needs the strength of central government, even if it entails the burden of officialdom.

Money

5:10 *He who loves money will not be satisfied with money; nor he who loves wealth, with gain: this also is vanity.*

11 *When goods increase, they increase who eat them; and what gain has their owner but to see them with his eyes?*

12 *Sweet is the sleep of a labourer, whether he eats little or much; but the surfeit of the rich will not let him sleep.*

The subject of these reflections is one of our most compelling interests, as Jesus implied when He warned us against making mammon a second God. The three sayings show it up for what it is, by pointing out the craving it creates, the hangers-on it attracts, and the dyspeptic plight which is its typical reward.

Verse 10 is a little classic on the love of money, a fit companion to the famous saying in 1 Timothy 6:9 f. on its moral and

[1] Delitzsch, *ad loc.*
[2] No translation of this verse (Heb. 8) has won general approval. Some commentators find in it praise of a king who, like Uzziah, loves farming (*cf.* NEB); others see the dependence of even a despot on the soil (*cf.* AV, RV, TEV). JB assumes too much with its rendering, 'You will hear talk of "the common good" and "the service of the king".' Some of these variations arise from the possibility of attaching the word 'served' either to 'king' or (in the sense of 'cultivated') to 'fields'. The Massoretic punctuation points to the latter.

spiritual harvest. Here the interest is psychological, though the final remark, *this also is vanity*, drives home the ultimate lesson to be learnt from it. The unappeased craving it creates is very obvious in the gambler, the tycoon and the well-paid materialist who never has enough—for the love of money grows by what it feeds on. But it may show itself more subtly in a general discontent: a longing not necessarily for more money but for inward fulfilment. If anything is worse than the addiction money brings, it is the emptiness it leaves. Man, with eternity in his heart, needs better nourishment than this.

The second saying of the three (verse 11) may have in mind not only the complex establishment that somehow grows with growing wealth, but the swarm of hangers-on. On these, there is a tragi-comic prophecy in Isaiah 22:23 ff., which promises a certain courtier high office, but warns him that he will find himself disastrously encumbered. 'They will hang on him the whole weight of his father's house,' place-hunters to a man; and the prophet, warming to his theme, pictures him as a peg with eventually half the contents of the kitchen hung on it—until peg and all come crashing down. But in our verse there is no such climax: only the irony of having to live on one's prestige and little else.

The third saying on money (12) is illustrated wherever affluence and indulgence join hands. Here the rich man is sleepless not with overwork, as in 2:23, or with strain, as one version would have it here ('he stays awake worrying', TEV). Merely with overeating.

Whatever discomforts the labourer puts up with, this will not be one of them; and whatever burdens were laid on Adam at the Fall, there was a rough mercy in the sentence, 'In the sweat of your face you shall eat bread.' We offer an unconscious comment on it by our modern exercise-machines and health clubs—for it is one of our human absurdities to pour out money and effort just to undo the damage of money and ease.

Ecclesiastes 5:13—6:12
The bitterness of disappointment

For the last chapter-and-a-half of Ecclesiastes we have been more concerned with living sensibly in the world as we find it—and this included the world of our religious obligations—than with wondering whether we are getting anywhere. The question has been there, reflected twice in the comment, 'This also is vanity' (4:16; 5:10); now it is again the centre of attention as Qoheleth names some of the bitter anomalies of life. He will end chapter 6, and with it the first half of his book, by pressing a question he had earlier seemed to answer: 'Who knows what is good for man ... under the sun?'

The crash

5:13 *There is a grievous evil which I have seen under the sun: riches were kept by their owner to his hurt,* [14] *and those riches were lost in a bad venture; and he is father of a son, but he has nothing in his hand.* [15] *As he came from his mother's womb he shall go again, naked as he came, and shall take nothing for his toil, which he may carry away in his hand.* [16] *This also is a grievous evil: just as he came, so shall he go; and what gain has he that he toiled for the wind,* [17] *and spent all his days in darkness and grief, in much vexation and sickness and resentment?*

A miniature case-history now brings us face to face with frustration—for this author prefers to show us samples from life rather than abstractions. Here, then, is a man who loses all his money at a single blow, leaving his family destitute. It might have made sense had it been the penalty of deals that were too smart—the 'wealth hastily gotten' which deserves to dwindle (Pr. 13:11)—or a miser's hoard[1] instead of a father's savings; or again, a gambling loss rather than a business failure.[2] But in fact it was toiled for and worried over; now it has spoilt his life twice over, first in the getting, then in the losing. And if his case is an extreme one, we all face something like it: we shall go out as naked as we arrived. 'It isn't right!'—such is TEV's reaction (16). Qoheleth's own is not quite as sweeping, for he is mainly pointing out what happens, not what ought to happen, in a world we can neither dictate to nor take root in. 'A deadly[3] evil' is perhaps the nearest we can get to his expression for it. That was how he introduced the matter (13); and he repeats it: 'a deadly evil . . .; and what gain has he that he toiled for the wind . . .?' (16)

At this point we have to be reminded that such a man may be asking of life more than it can give. If his plans were made just on the strength of what lay within reach and what promised some security, he was looking in the wrong direction. So the final paragraph will put us right, talking of life now in very different terms.

A more excellent way

5:18 *Behold, what I have seen to be good and to be fitting is to eat and drink and find enjoyment in all the toil with which one toils under the sun the few days of his life which God has given him, for this is his lot.* [19] *Every man also to whom God has given wealth and possessions and power to enjoy them, and to accept his lot and find enjoyment in his toil —this is the gift of God.* [20] *For he will not much remember the days of his life because God keeps him occupied with joy in his heart.*

At first sight this may look like the mere praise of simplicity and moderation; but in fact the key word is God, and the secret of life held out to us is openness to Him: a readiness to take what comes to us as heaven-sent, whether it is toil or wealth or both. This is more than *good and . . . fitting* (18): more literally it is 'a good thing which is beautiful'. Once more, a positive note has broken through, and as the chapter ends we catch a glimpse of the man for whom life passes swiftly, not because it is short and

[1] *Cf.* Pr. 11:24-26 on its unhappy influence; 28:22 on its transience.
[2] *Venture* (14) does not imply unnecessary risk; it is the word translated 'business' in 1:13; 3:10; 5:3 (Heb. 2), *etc.*
[3] Lit. 'sick'. It implies trouble that is distressing and deep-seated.

58

meaningless but because, by the grace of God, he finds it utterly absorbing. This will be the theme of the closing chapters; but first there is more to be explored of human experience and its harsh realities.

Tantalization

6:1 *There is an evil which I have seen under the sun, and it lies heavy upon men:* [2] *a man to whom God gives wealth, possessions, and honour, so that he lacks nothing of all that he desires, yet God does not give him power to enjoy them, but a stranger enjoys them; this is vanity; it is a sore affliction.* [3] *If a man begets a hundred children, and lives many years, so that the days of his years are many, but he does not enjoy life's good things, and also has no burial, I say that an untimely birth is better off than he.* [4] *For it comes into vanity and goes into darkness, and in darkness its name is covered;* [5] *moreover it has not seen the sun or known anything; yet it finds rest rather than he.* [6] *Even though he should live a thousand years twice told, yet enjoy no good—do not all go to the one place?*

At once we are faced with the fact that the *power to enjoy* God's gifts, which was held before us in 5:19, is itself a gift which may or may not be allotted us. There are more ways than one of being deprived of it. There was the business collapse of 5:13 ff., where everything had been sacrificed to a future which never materialized. For that man the dawn never came. But life can have long spells of brilliance and joy, and still succumb to darkness, which will seem all the deeper for the light it has quenched. The man of verse 2, just because he is outstanding, has more to lose than the plodder who will never arrive. And he may well lose it through no fault of his own: perhaps when war, or sickness, or injustice spills everything into another's lap. If he is tantalized, so are those who have outward wealth and inward poverty—for the trouble is not simply that some possessions are less satisfying than others, as undoubtedly they are, or that they are given meagrely. One could have the things men dream of—which in Old Testament terms meant children by the score, and years of life by the thousand—and still depart unnoticed, unlamented [4] and unfulfilled.

At this point we may protest that life is not by any means as black as this for most people. Normally we can take the rough

---

[4] This is the force of *has no burial* (6:3): see Je. 22:18 f.

with the smooth, and find our life decidedly worth living. This of course is true, and is thoroughly well founded if we are men of faith like those we met at the end of chapter five. Even if we are not, we may still live contentedly, as thousands do, and not be worried about the ultimate meaning of things.

To this, Qoheleth might reply, first, that he is speaking here of some people, not all; and secondly that if we ourselves are not concerned about meanings and values, somebody should be—and who are we to opt out of that responsibility? Once more he is inviting us to think, and in particular to think through the secularist's position. If this life is all, and offers to some people frustration rather than fulfilment, leaving them nothing to pass on to those who depend on them; if, further, all alike are waiting their turn to be deleted (6c), then some indeed can envy the stillborn, whose turn comes first. Job and Jeremiah, at times, would have fervently agreed (Jb. 3; Je. 20:14 ff.); and if we disagree with that mood of those two men, it is because we judge their lives by values that transcend death and outweigh a lifetime's pains and pleasures—criteria that the secularist cannot logically use.

All this is damaging to any rosy picture of the world; but TEV goes far beyond its brief in calling it 'a serious injustice . . . done to man' (6:1), and in making 6:2 say, 'it just isn't right'.[5] Qoheleth is very far from holding that man has rights which God ignores; it is rather that man has needs which God exposes. Some of these, as we saw, are of a kind that the temporal world cannot begin to meet, since God has 'put eternity into man's mind' (3:11); others, more limited, are of a kind that the world can satisfy a little and for a while; but none with any certainty or depth. If this is a hardship and *lies heavy upon men* (1), it is also a salutary thing. The world itself is made to say to us, in the only language we will mostly listen to, 'This is no place to rest.'[6]

But we are, for the moment, not encouraged to glean any wisdom from it, for in itself the human rat-race makes no sense at all.

---

[5] The OT can use the word for *an evil* (6:1) in a neutral sense, to denote hardship or disaster: *cf.*, *e.g.*, Is. 45:7 ('woe'); Am. 3:6 ('does evil befall a city . . .?'). Similarly *good* in this passage is well translated 'enjoyment' and 'life's good things' (5:18; 6:3). The last phrase of verse 2, so far from meaning 'it isn't right' (TEV), is lit. 'it is a bad sickness'; hence RSV, *a sore affliction.*

[6] Mi. 2:10.

So the chapter will wind its way down to a depressing and uncertain finish, well suited to the state of man on his own.

Unanswered questions

6:7 *All the toil of man is for his mouth, yet his appetite is not satisfied.*
8 *For what advantage has the wise man over the fool? And what does the poor man have who knows how to conduct himself before the living?*
9 *Better is the sight of the eyes than the wandering of desire; this also is vanity and a striving after wind.*

10 *Whatever has come to be has already been named, and it is known what man is, and that he is not able to dispute with one stronger than he.*
11 *The more words, the more vanity, and what is man the better?* 12 *For who knows what is good for man while he lives the few days of his vain life, which he passes like a shadow? For who can tell man what will be after him under the sun?*

The thoughts and questions of the chapter's final paragraph pick up some issues that have met us earlier, to substantiate the motto of the book, 'Vanity of vanities!'

The first of them (7) makes a point which is as real to modern man on his industrial treadmill as to the primitive peasant scraping a bare living from the soil: that he works to eat, for the strength to go on working to go on eating. Even if he enjoys his work—and his food—the compulsion is still there. His mouth, not his mind, seems to be master.

When we object that men have more in them than this, and better things to live for, verse 8 does not let this pass without a challenge. Wisdom, for example, may be infinitely better than folly, as an earlier passage remarked (2:13), but is the wise man better-off than the fool? Materially he may or may not be, though surely he deserves to be; and we have seen already that death will level the two of them with complete indifference.[7] As for happiness, the wise man's clarity of vision is not all joy: 'For in much wisdom', as 1:18 puts it, 'is much vexation, and he who increases knowledge increases sorrow.'

As if sensing that we may still be unconvinced, since we rate the quality of a man's life higher than its comforts, Qoheleth asks the hard-headed question of 8b: What does a poor man, however

[7] Ec. 2:14 ff.

well thought of,[8] actually get for his pains? It is a fair question. To reverse one of R. L. Stevenson's familiar sayings, to arrive is, for most of us, better than to travel hopefully. That is the force of verse 9a, and its common sense allows us no daydreams. The trouble is that to 'arrive' is—in any ultimate and satisfying sense —beyond our power. Whatever we achieve will melt away as *vanity and a striving after wind*, whether it is the poor man's self-help or the rich man's success.

Is this defeatism or realism? In terms of life 'under the sun' it is wholly realistic, as the argument of the book has already shown. Whatever brave words we may multiply about man, or against his Maker, verses 10 and 11 remind us that we shall not alter the way in which we and our world were made. These things are already *named* and *known* (10), which is another way of saying, with the rest of Scripture, that they owe their being to the command of God; and this command now includes the sentence passed at Adam's fall. Naturally we find it hard, and want to protest. The idea of disputing with the Almighty (10b, 11) fascinated Job, who abandoned it only after much heart-searching;[9] it earned its classic rebuke in Isaiah 45:9 ff., with the picture of the clay offering officious advice to the potter. Yet we still find it easier to enlarge on the way things ought to have been than to face the truth of what they are.

But this truth, to be the whole truth, must include what they are becoming, and what will become of us. Part of this, that we shall die, we know all too well; the rest, all too little. So the chapter, at this mid-point of the book, ends with a string of unanswered questions. Secular man, heading for death, and swept along by change, can only echo, '*Who knows what is good . . .? Who can tell man what will be after him . . .?*'

It is a double bewilderment. He is left with no absolute values to live for ('what is good?'); not even any practical certainties ('what will be?') to plan for.

[8] The expression, 'who knows how to walk . . .', may imply either a morally or a socially well-conducted life. The word used for *poor* is one which elsewhere tends to mark the downtrodden who look to God for help.

[9] See, *e.g.*, Jb. chapters 9, 13 and 23; also 31:35-37; 42:1-6.

A second summary
A backward glance over Ecclesiastes 4:9—6:12

In our first summary (page 48) we were reminded how widely the opening chapters had ranged in search of a satisfying end in life. Then, for a while, the quest appeared to have been called off. From 4:9 to about 5:12 we could pause to look around and study the human scene with some detachment. The comments were as keen as ever, but the tone was cool, almost acquiescent.

Yet this was irony, not acceptance. From 5:13 onwards we were no longer spared the disquiet that the world's anomalies and tragedies should arouse in us. We sampled its searing disappointments: the sudden ruin of a life's work (5:13–17); the glittering achievements that brought no happiness (6:1–6). There was a glimpse of better things at the close of chapter 5, a token that Qoheleth would lead us to an answer in the end; but the relief was short-lived. Chapter 6, which started by exposing a few empty lives, went on to uncover our human ant-hill, endlessly and meaninglessly busy (6:7–9), and finished by dismissing our fine speeches about progress (6:10–12). For all his talk, man on his own has no ability to change himself; no permanence; not even anywhere to make for.

Ecclesiastes 7:1–22

Interlude: More reflections, maxims and home truths

With his sure touch the author now brings in a stimulating change
of style and approach. Instead of reflecting and arguing, he will
bombard us with proverbs, with their strong impact and varied
angles of attack. The opening ones are provocatively cheerless;
the rest (for the most part) provocatively cool and canny.

You may as well face facts!

7:1 *A good name is better than precious ointment;*
     and the day of death, than the day of birth.
  2 *It is better to go to the house of mourning*
     than to go to the house of feasting;
   for this is the end of all men,
     and the living will lay it to heart.
  3 *Sorrow is better than laughter,*
     for by sadness of countenance the heart is made glad.
  4 *The heart of the wise is in the house of mourning;*
     but the heart of fools is in the house of mirth.
  5 *It is better for a man to hear the rebuke of the wise*
     than to hear the song of fools.
  6 *For as the crackling of thorns under a pot,*
     so is the laughter of fools;
     this also is vanity.

Nothing in the first half of verse 1 prepares us for the body-blow
of the second half. There was something like it in the previous
chapter (6:1–6), but that was speaking of special cases. This saying is so sweeping and so contrary to the normal outlook, that

64

we must either take a leap into the New Testament, where 'to depart and be with Christ' is seen to be 'far better' than to stay (but Ecclesiastes has already refused to presuppose a future life, in 3:21), or else we must read on and hope for clarification in the verses that follow.

This, sure enough, we find; and it is spelt out most clearly at the end of the next verse, especially in the saying, *and the living will lay it to heart*. In other words, *the day of death* has more to teach us than *the day of birth*; its lessons are more factual and, paradoxically, more vital. At a birth (and, to draw on the next few verses, on all festive and gay occasions) the general mood is excited and expansive. It is no time for dwelling on life's brevity or on human limitations: we let our fancies and our hopes run high. At *the house of mourning*, on the other hand, the mood is thoughtful and the facts are plain. If we shrug them off, it is our fault: we shall have no better chance of facing them. The great psalm of human mortality, Psalm 90, puts it with majestic simplicity:

> 'So teach us to number our days
> that we may get a heart of wisdom.'

Like the psalm, this passage has a positive result in view, which is clear from its insistence on the word *better*, and especially from the last part of verse 3, whether we translate it with RSV,[1] *by sadness of countenance the heart is made glad*, or with AV, '. . . the heart is made better'.[2] The thought of sadness being not only replaced by joy but being in itself a preparation for the truest form of it—unlike the hectic, empty gaiety of fools, quick to catch alight, quick to fade[3]—is most memorably put in John 16:20 ff., using the analogy of childbirth, whose pains prepare the way for special joy. In other terms, *cf.* 2 Corinthians 4:17 f. and, in the Old Testament, Job 33:19-30.

[1] *Cf.* RV; also, less realistically, NEB ('a sad face may go with a cheerful heart').

[2] TEV, 'it sharpens your understanding', takes 'heart' as the equivalent of 'mind', which is often the case in the OT. But the Heb. expression found here is a standard one for feeling cheerful. *Cf.*, *e.g.*, Ru. 3:7.

[3] Verse 6 makes a pun on the two senses of the Heb. *sîr*, 'thorn' and 'pot'.

65

You may as well be rational!

7:7 *Surely oppression makes the wise man foolish,*
and a bribe corrupts the mind.
8 *Better is the end of a thing than its beginning;*
and the patient in spirit is better than the proud in spirit.
9 *Be not quick to anger,*
for anger lodges in the bosom of fools.
10 *Say not, 'Why were the former days better than these?'*
For it is not from wisdom that you ask this.
11 *Wisdom is good with an inheritance,*
an advantage to those who see the sun.
12 *For the protection of wisdom is like the protection of money;*
and the advantage of knowledge is that wisdom preserves the
life of him who has it.
13 *Consider the work of God;*
who can make straight what he has made crooked?

14 *In the day of prosperity be joyful, and in the day of adversity con-*
sider; God has made the one as well as the other, so that man may not
find out anything that will be after him.

15 *In my vain life I have seen everything; there is a righteous man who*
perishes in his righteousness, and there is a wicked man who prolongs his
life in his evil-doing. 16 *Be not righteous overmuch, and do not make your-*
self overwise; why should you destroy yourself? 17 *Be not wicked overmuch,*
neither be a fool; why should you die before your time? 18 *It is good that*
you should take hold of this, and from that withhold not your hand; for he
who fears God shall come forth from them all.

19 *Wisdom gives strength to the wise man more than ten rulers that*
are in a city.

20 *Surely there is not a righteous man on earth who does good and*
never sins.

21 *Do not give heed to all the things that men say, lest you hear your*
servant cursing you; 22 *your heart knows that many times you have your-*
self cursed others.

There are almost as many moods and standpoints here as there are
sayings, but a certain low-key approach to the subject marks most
of them. Meeting the man of the world on his own not very
exalted ground, Qoheleth points out that there are self-evident
advantages in trying to make sense of life, instead of relapsing
into cynicism or despair.

In verse 7 we can recognize the essence of a law which, in modern times, Lord Acton formulated as 'All power tends to corrupt . . .'. It is interesting that the implied appeal here is to one's self-respect, for no-one willingly makes a real fool of himself—which is what the cruel or corrupt official is doing by definition, since he acts without reference to the merits of a case. His mind has been tampered with: it is now the tool of avarice or spite, not the servant of truth.

Taking verses 8 and 9 together, we are again shown the purely foolish side of attitudes which the moralist would condemn on weightier grounds, but grounds which make little appeal to the worldly man. Whether or not we regard patience as a virtue and quarrelsomeness as a vice, we can at least see the practical good sense of self-control: of following a matter through instead of dropping it at the first affront to our dignity. It is not the only kind of area in which the wrong course can also be deflatingly described as the childish one.

Verse 10 is even more crushing, as befits an answer to nostalgia, which is an enervating and self-indulgent mood. To sigh for 'the good old days' is (we may reflect) doubly unrealistic: a substitute not only for action but for proper thought, since it almost invariably overlooks the evils that took a different form or vexed a different section of society in other times. The clear-eyed Qoheleth is the last person to be impressed by this golden haze around the past: he has already declared that one age is very much like another. 'What has been is what will be, . . . and there is nothing new under the sun' (1:9). All this, he now implies, is too obvious to be worth arguing: he need only ask us to talk more sensibly.

There follows in verses 11 and 12 an unusually mundane estimate of wisdom. There is some doubt as to the right translation, but little doubt that *wisdom* is, for the moment, being treated on much the same footing as *money*, for its utility value: a comparable or an added insurance against the risks of life.[4] If so, it is hardly a flattering comparison for something whose true worth is incalculable, according to Proverbs 8:11 and many other passages. Verse 12b may be claiming that wisdom, unlike money, is life-

---

[4] Verse 11 may mean that to have both wealth and wisdom is a double boon (AV, RSV); but probably the expression *good with* means 'as good as' (RV, TEV): cf. the Heb. of, e.g., 2:16b; Jb. 37:18, where 'like' is lit. 'with'. NEB deletes a consonant to obtain the sense, 'better than'.

giving;[5] but it would be in keeping with the modest aims of this passage if no more than its practical, protective value were in mind. The phrase in 11b, *an advantage to those who see the sun,* may well be a double-edged remark, a reminder that there is a time-limit to the help that even wisdom, at this level of general good sense, can offer. It pays no dividends in the grave.

The rest of these assorted sayings, continuing to verse 22, show how variable is the advice of common sense when it has no unifying principle. It will swing from pious resignation to moral cynicism (13-18); and it will note the flaws in human nature yet be chiefly concerned with managing to live with them (20-22).

To look at these sayings in a little more detail: verse 13 is speaking not of moral crookedness but of the shapes of things and events which we find awkward but should accept from God. It includes His judgments—for 'the way of the wicked he "twists"', as Psalm 146:9 literally puts it (using this verb)—but also presumably many of life's trials, as the next verse (14) suggests. That verse is a little classic on the right approach to good times and bad, which is to accept both from God for what they can give: not with the Stoic's impassiveness, nor with the restlessness of those who cannot bring themselves to accept a bonus with delight, or a blow with an open and reflective mind.

'Take what He gives,
And praise Him still,
Through good or ill,
Who ever lives.'[6]

But true to his theme, Qoheleth must underline the mystery of what God sends, and especially the unpredictability of it, which clips the wings of our self-sufficiency. It is the point already made in 3:11, where time and eternity, obscurity and clarity, tantalize and beckon us, in case we should imagine ourselves to be either no more than cattle or no less than gods.

Now comes the cynicism, in verses 15-18: the shabby and self-regarding side of common sense. To show us the logic of the

[5] The single word translated *preserves the life of* can also mean 'gives life to' or 'revives', according to its contexts. *Cf., e.g.,* 1 Sa. 2:6; Ps. 85:6 (Heb. 7). And 'life' in the OT, as in the NT, often means spiritual vitality not merely physical existence.
[6] Richard Baxter, 'Ye holy angels bright'.

secular position Qoheleth shuts out for a while any gleam of genuine faith, and introduces religion at the end only in the form of superstition, which would reduce God to the status of an indemnity clause.

Revealingly enough, while verse 15 can be matched and out-matched in the musings of Job, who paints evocative pictures of the tranquil sinner and the tormented saint in such chapters as 21 and 30–31, Job never draws the abject conclusions that are presented in our verses 16 ff. He would rather die than renounce his claim to righteousness, even if to uphold it were to challenge heaven itself. 'Behold, he will slay me; I have no hope; yet I will defend my ways to his face.'[7]

By the side of that spirited resolve, the motto, 'nothing to excess', has never looked so cheap as in these verses, which recommend moral cowardice with so straight a face that we are forced to take them seriously for the moment. In doing so, we realize that it is indeed the morality, acknowledged or unacknowledged, of the worldly man if he is true to his beliefs. We could add that in our present society it is becoming more and more openly the norm. Verse 18 plumbs the depths, advocating, a little cryptically,[8] not mere half-heartedness in good or evil but a generous mixture of the two, since religion will take care of any risks, and one will therefore enjoy the best of both life-styles.

After this, the unexceptionable statement of verse 19 restores a little of our confidence in the value of good sense (though not, perhaps, in the value of politicians). Even with regard to wisdom, a later saying (9:16) will remind us not to expect too much recognition for a quality so intangible.

Isolated from the cynicism of verses 16–18, verse 20 can be taken at its face value, as a confession, not an excuse. There is no shrug of the shoulders as we say it, as the earlier verses would have implied; yet the next piece of common sense perhaps draws the sting of the admission a little. In itself, 21 f. is excellent advice, since to take too seriously what people say of us is asking to get hurt, and in any case we have all said some wounding things in our time. But perhaps the three verses, 20–22, together take our failings a little more casually than is usual in Scripture,

---

[7] Jb. 13:15; cf., e.g., 27:1–6.
[8] *This* and *that* would be more clearly rendered 'the one' and 'the other', *i.e.*, righteousness and wickedness. The final line is well paraphrased by TEV: 'If you fear God you will be successful anyway.'

and we may still be listening here to Mr Sensible (to borrow a name from C. S. Lewis)[9] rather than to the authentic voice of wisdom. Certainly Qoheleth finds no point of rest in any of these maxims: he is deeply dissatisfied with their shallowness, as his next words show.

[9] C. S. Lewis, *The Pilgrim's Regress* (2nd ed., Bles, 1943), pp. 82 ff.

Ecclesiastes 7:23–29
The search goes on

7:23 All this I have tested by wisdom; I said, 'I will be wise'; but it was far from me. 24 That which is, is far off, and deep, very deep; who can find it out? 25 I turned my mind to know and to search out and to seek wisdom and the sum of things, and to know the wickedness of folly and the foolishness which is madness. 26 And I found more bitter than death the woman whose heart is snares and nets, and whose hands are fetters; he who pleases God escapes her, but the sinner is taken by her. 27 Behold, this is what I found, says the Preacher, adding one thing to another to find the sum, 28 which my mind has sought repeatedly, but I have not found. One man among a thousand I found, but a woman among all these I have not found. 29 Behold, this alone I found, that God made man upright, but they have sought out many devices.

The honest admission of failure to find wisdom—of watching it in fact recede with every step one takes, discovering that none of our soundings ever gets to the bottom of things—this is, if not the beginning of wisdom, a good path to that beginning. After the ambitious quest of chapter 2, the search has moved to less exotic areas, delving into common experience, pausing at times to see what can be made of life from day to day, whatever its ultimate secrets. At this level the findings may have been shrewd enough, even too shrewd. But *tested by wisdom* (23), which looks for answers to the question, 'What is life *about*?', they have given not the ghost of a reply.

So the confession of 7:23 f. has a devastating finality. It could be the epitaph of every philosopher, and we can set it out in that form, suitably urn-shaped:

> I said,
> 'I will be wise';
> but it was far from me.
> That which is, is far off,
> and deep, very deep;
> who can find it out?

Like any unanswered question, this riddle about life had been a stimulus at first. The series of verbs, *to know . . . to search out . . . to seek* (25), conveys the eagerness of the quest, as Edgar Jones points out.[1] But it is part of man's condition that though he may formulate his task in terms of detached enquiry and philosophizing—seeking a total account of things,[2] and aware of evil as folly and madness[3]—he must turn also to the sphere of human relationships in his search for the world's meaning, yet see them necessarily through the distorting lens of sin. So our author startles us with his bitter verdict: that he has found only one man in a thousand who was not a disappointment, but not a single woman. How are we to take this?

For a start, we should notice that he is not dogmatizing but reporting. This is one man's experience, and he does not universalize it.[4] But what is more to the point is that he exposes to us the part that sin can play on both sides of an encounter between the sexes. A deeply disillusioning entanglement like that of verse 26 can distort, even destroy, any subsequent attempt at relationship. No doubt Qoheleth made his escape, as he may imply in 26b, but not undamaged. His fruitless search for a woman he could trust may tell us as much about him and his approach, as about any of his acquaintances. It is tempting to add—and could conceivably be relevant—that like Solomon, whose mantle he has worn before,[5] he might have done better to have cast his net less widely than among 'a thousand'! He almost says as much in 9:9, with his praise of simple marital fidelity.

In the last verse of chapter 7 he gives us a firmer conclusion on

[1] Jones, p. 321.
[2] *The sum* (25, 27) could be translated 'the reckoning', with something of both senses of that term: *i.e.*, the 'total' and the 'rationale' of things (*cf.* McNeile).
[3] Verse 25b is best translated '. . . that wickedness is folly, and that foolishness is madness' (RV).
[4] Verse 20, by contrast, shows that he does not shrink from universalizations where they are appropriate.
[5] See the opening comments on the section 1:12—2:26 (p. 28).

human nature than he could reach by bare experience. He turns to what has been revealed, drawing evidently on Genesis 1-3. To appreciate the importance of this biblical view of God and man, we have only to hear the account of the matter given in the Babylonian Theodicy, where it is the gods who are responsible for the wickedness of men: 'With lies, and not truth, they endowed them for ever.'[6] That view is paralysing, for virtue is costly enough without the added suspicion that it has no truth on its side, that in fact it goes against all that is most human. Incidentally, it is not confined to ancient Babylon. In practice it is the view—without the theology—of all who believe that to be *upright* (29) is to be naïve and less than adult.

That suspicion and that view, we are reminded here, go back to the Fall, but not to our beginnings. After the gropings of this chapter, this verse brings the refreshing certainty that our *many devices*—our clouding of moral issues, our refusal of the straight way—are our fault, not our fate. It is bad enough to have spoilt what was flawless; that is guilt. But to have been a mere part in what was meaningless would have spelt despair. The words, *God made man upright*, even though they have their tragic sequel, are already enough to call in question the refrain, 'Vanity of vanities'. Since futility was not the first word about our world, it no longer has to be the last.

[6] 'The Babylonian Theodicy', line 280, in W. G. Lambert, *Babylonian Wisdom Literature* (Clarendon, Oxford, 1960), p. 89.

Ecclesiastes 8:1–17
Frustration

At every turn this chapter will face us with our inability to call
the tune and master our affairs. On one level after another we find
ourselves pinned down, hunted down and disorientated.

Force majeure

8:1 *Who is like the wise man?*
And who knows the interpretation of a thing?
A man's wisdom makes his face shine,
and the hardness of his countenance is changed.
2 *Keep the king's command, and because of your sacred oath be not*
dismayed; 3 *go from his presence, do not delay when the matter is un-*
pleasant, for he does whatever he pleases. 4 *For the word of the king is*
supreme, and who may say to him, 'What are you doing?' 5 *He who*
obeys a command will meet no harm, and the mind of a wise man will know
the time and way. 6 *For every matter has its time and way, although man's*
trouble lies heavy upon him. 7 *For he does not know what is to be, for*
who can tell him how it will be? 8 *No man has power to retain the spirit,*
or authority over the day of death; there is no discharge from war, nor
will wickedness deliver those who are given to it. 9 *All this I observed*
while applying my mind to all that is done under the sun, while man lords
it over man to his hurt.

Perhaps, as many think, Qoheleth has borrowed a familiar tag for
his opening verse in praise of wisdom and the wise. But with the
dangerous caprices of a king to reckon with, wisdom has to fold
its wings and take the form of discretion, content to keep its
possessor out of trouble. It is only the first of its frustrations, and

74

the smallest of them: there is at least something useful it can do in such a setting, whereas later in the chapter it will be faced with problems as intractable as death, moral perversity and the mystery of divine government.

Discretion, then, is the chief face of wisdom in this situation, though verse 1a, with its reminder of Joseph and Daniel, of Ahithophel and Hushai,[1] emphasizes the part that a more positive talent of the wise, *the interpretation of a thing*, should play at court. With that exception, wisdom is a demure and self-effacing figure in this paragraph, and we can reflect on the folly of a king, or any leader, whose contempt or fear of truth reduces her to silence by ensuring that the thoughtful keep their thoughts to themselves.

Cautious as the wise man must be, he is not being pressed here to give up his integrity. His readiness to please need not be servile. The lively, pleasant expression of his face, which verse 1b points out, is not put on for effect: it does indeed express him, the person he is and the cast of his mind. There is principle, too, not time-serving, in his obedience, a fact brought out in RV's accurate translation of verse 2: '. . . Keep the king's command, and that in regard of the oath of God.'[2] It is within that framework that he also uses his wits, as a wise man should,[3] to size up a perilous situation (3)[4] and judge the timing of his actions (5b, 6a). Many passages in the Old Testament witness to the limits which loyalty to God must set on courtly tact and submissiveness; one has only to think of the outspoken prophets and, among the wise, of the indomitable Daniel and his companions. If such examples shame us out of conformism, the present verses keep the balance true by teaching due respect for government. The New Testament

---

[1] 2 Sa. 16:20—17:14.

[2] The verse ends here in MT. Whether the oath of God is God's legitimation of the king, or the subject's oath of loyalty (either is possible), it puts the matter in any case on a religious footing. The fact that obedience pays (5) is an additional incentive, which the NT also considers worth mentioning (Rom. 13:3–5).

[3] *Cf.*, *e.g.*, Pr. 14:15 f.; 22:3.

[4] Verse 3, which begins in MT with RSV's 2c, *be not dismayed* (or, 'Be not precipitate'), is difficult. The opening may advise against holding high office (RSV, NEB, TEV), or against an impulsive relinquishing of it (Barton, Jones). Its syntax is ambiguous. The last two clauses may mean, *do not delay, etc.*, as in RSV, but are perhaps better understood with JB as 'do not be stubborn when the cause is not a good one'.

in the same way will give prominence now to one side of the matter, now to the other.[5]

The mention of *the time and way*[6] (5, 6) which the wise man learns to recognize—the truth and the moment of truth which may be seized or missed in any venture—recalls the theme of chapter 3, with its glimpses of a time-conditioned, ever-changing world. There we were groping for something permanent; here, for something predictable (7). It is cold comfort to find only death in this category; and little better, as one recoils from the prospect, to be confronted by the present which is full of suffering, *while man lords it over man to his hurt* (9). There is special irony in that last remark, where the rather striking word for man's abuse of power (*lords it*) looks back pointedly to what has just been said about his impotence in other respects: his inability to hold his own spirit captive,[7] or to lord it over death—for a single family of lordly words colours all these statements. The rest of verse 8, especially in TEV's paraphrase, puts the last encounter in vivid terms: 'That is a battle we cannot escape; we cannot cheat our way out.'

Moral perversity

8:10 *Then I saw the wicked buried; they used to go in and out of the holy place, and were praised in the city where they had done such things. This also is vanity.* [11] *Because sentence against an evil deed is not executed speedily, the heart of the sons of men is fully set to do evil.* [12] *Though a sinner does evil a hundred times and prolongs his life, yet I know that it will be well with those who fear God, because they fear before him;* [13] *but it will not be well with the wicked, neither will he prolong his days like a shadow, because he does not fear before God.*

There are few things more obnoxious than the sight of wicked men flourishing and complacent. Yet wickedness respected and

---

[5] *E.g.*, Mt. 23:2, 3a, in counterpoint with the rest of that chapter. *Cf.* 1 Pet. 2:13 ff. with Acts 5:29.

[6] Alternatively it may be right to understand *way* (5 f.) and *trouble* (6) in their primary senses, as 'judgment' and 'evil'. In that case (as Delitzsch points out) the passage will be making the point that the wise man will wait God's time for judgment, and will not take matters into his own hands by rebellion.

[7] The Heb. word for the spirit serves also for the wind, which is proverbially uncontrollable (*cf.* Pr. 27:16); *cf.* JB, NEB, here. But spirit is more directly relevant at this point.

given the blessing of religion (10a)[8] is even more sickening. In the spectacle described here, the sycophants have not even the excuse of ignorance. The villains are being honoured at the very scene of their misdeeds—and they are no longer alive to cast their spell of fear or favour over anyone. So, incredibly enough, the admiration must be genuine, making it very clear that popular moral judgments can be totally astray, swayed by the evidence of success or failure, and construing heaven's patience as its approval. The dictator or the corrupt tycoon may have bent the rules, it will be said; but after all, they got things done, they had flair, they lived in style.

This is too much for Qoheleth. He is stung into one of his rare declarations of his own faith, dropping the veil of secularism which he normally adopts for the sake of the discussion. It has happened before (see on 2:26; 3:17; 5:18–20; 7:14), and in the final chapters it will be no longer the exception but the rule.

What he certainly affirms here is judgment. In the end, the right thing will be done in every case. *It will be well with those who fear God . . .; but it will not be well with the wicked.* What he may also be faintly raising in our minds is the thought of an after-life for the godly. If so, he does it by an unresolved paradox about the wicked—for in the same breath he tells of the villain both prolonging and failing to prolong his life (12, 13). This could mean that whereas the godly man has hope beyond the grave, the ungodly has none: however long postponed, death will be the end for him. This is the way some of the Psalms unfold the matter.[9]

Yet Qoheleth's refusal to pronounce on this elsewhere, contenting himself with the question, 'Who knows?' (3:21), makes it more likely that he is generalizing here. Wickedness, he declares, brings no true benefits (13a); and as a rule—however striking the exceptions (12, 14)—it riddles life with insecurity. The wicked man's career is all show, no substance.[1]

[8] Verse 10 is far from clear to us, but NEB has no textual warrant for changing 'buried' (*qbrym*) to 'approaching' (*qrbym*). On the other hand, there is overwhelming support in the ancient versions (and many MSS) for reading 'praised' (√*šbḥ*) rather than 'forgotten' (√*škḥ*, MT, cf. AV, RV).

[9] E.g., Pss. 49:14 f.; 73:18 ff.

[1] The clause about the *shadow* in verse 13 should probably be understood as 'prolong his days, which are like a shadow'; cf., e.g., 6:12; Pss. 102:11; 109:23, etc. Less probably, it could picture the lengthening of shadows at evening; but that kind of 'prolonging' heralds rather than postpones the approach of night.

Small expectations

8:14 *There is a vanity which takes place on earth, that there are righteous men to whom it happens according to the deeds of the wicked, and there are wicked men to whom it happens according to the deeds of the righteous. I said that this also is vanity.* [15] *And I commend enjoyment, for man has no good thing under the sun but to eat, and drink, and enjoy himself, for this will go with him in his toil through the days of life which God gives him under the sun.*

A moment ago we were reminded of the general rule that wickedness digs its own grave, and righteousness, so to speak, its own garden. But all too often the pattern reverses, to make nonsense[2] of itself; for there is no sure way of knowing when—let alone why—life will rain down on us the next blow or the next windfall. Moral effort may pay no dividends at all, and while this may make it all the nobler, it is only natural to look for a safer kind of investment. In those terms—which in verse 15 are twice underlined by the words, *under the sun*—the simple satisfactions are the soundest. It is not the first time we have been brought back to them, nor the last; but Qoheleth never overvalues them. Always he partners them with some reminder of the darker side of life (here, its *toil*), which they can only mitigate.

The riddle remains

8:16 *When I applied my mind to know wisdom, and to see the business that is done on earth, how neither day nor night one's eyes see sleep;* [17] *then I saw all the work of God, that man cannot find out the work that is done under the sun. However much man may toil in seeking, he will not find it out; even though a wise man claims to know, he cannot find it out.*

If we needed reminding that hard work and simple living can only shelve our ultimate questions, never settle them, this sequel to the bland advice of verse 15 should be enough. The very busyness[3] of life worries us into asking where it is taking us, and

---

[2] TEV, however, applies the word 'nonsense' to the statement of verses 12 f., after changing the affirmation, 'I know . . .' (12) into the dismissive remark, 'I know what they say'. This is ingenious, but it is not the text.

[3] The sleeplessness of 16b is taken by TEV to be the thinker's as he wrestles with the problem. But it is more straightforward to translate it with reference to the people he observes.

what it means, if it does mean anything. We hardly need Qoheleth to point out that this is the very question that defeats us.
The world's long history of philosophies, each one in turn exposing the omissions of its predecessors, makes it all too clear.

But Qoheleth does point it out—and gives us a ray of hope by
the way he puts it. For it is *God's* work that baffles us (17): it is
not 'a tale told by an idiot'.

Yet what if it is told *to* an idiot? The chapter seems to end on
such a note. It allows our wisest men no prospect of success.
Nevertheless we pick up its meaning better if we catch the allusion in verse 17a to the great statement of 3:11. There too we
faced our narrowness of knowledge, but saw that eternity as
well as time has access to our minds. Although as time-dwellers
we see God's work in tantalizing flashes, the very fact that we
can ask about the whole design and long to see it, is evidence
that we are not entirely prisoners of our world.

In more promising words, it is evidence of not only how but
for Whom we have been made.

Ecclesiastes 9:1–18
Jeopardy

Before the positive emphasis of the final three chapters can emerge, we have to make sure that we shall be building on nothing short of hard reality. In case we should be cherishing some comforting illusions, chapter 9 confronts us with the little that we know, then with the vast extent of what we cannot handle: in particular, with death, the ups and downs of fortune, and the erratic favours of the crowd. But first it asks the crucial question, whether we are in the hands of friend or foe.

Is it love or hate?

9:1 *But all this I laid to heart, examining it all, how the righteous and the wise and their deeds are in the hand of God; whether it is love or hate man does not know.*

We have only to use our eyes without prejudice, according to Psalm 19 and Romans 1:19 ff., to see that there is a powerful and glorious Creator. But it takes more than observation to discover how He is disposed towards us. Whether we take the words *love or hate* here to be a biblical way of saying 'acceptance or rejection', or to have their simple, primary sense, we shall have, either way, only an uncertain answer about the Creator's character from the world we live in, with its mixture of delight and terror, beauty and repulsiveness.[1]

[1] Conceivably, however, verse 1b could be speaking of human rather than divine attitudes: *cf.* JB, 'Man does not know what love is, or hate'. Delitzsch and a few others, including TEV, infer from 1a that man is not sufficiently master of himself to know whether he will feel love or hate in a given situation (though not denying that he is responsible to accept or reject the feeling

If the question were left exactly poised it would still be unsettling; and all the more so, the more completely we felt ourselves to be in the enigmatic *hand of God* (1a). But Qoheleth now makes matters worse for us by pointing to one fact that seems to tip the scales decisively against us—always supposing that we are reasoning only by what we see. Then, for good measure, he faces us with two of its companion facts before he ends the chapter. The first of the three is death.

Death

9:1 *Everything before them is vanity,* [2] *since one fate comes to all, to the righteous and the wicked, to the good and the evil, to the clean and the unclean, to him who sacrifices and him who does not sacrifice. As is the good man, so is the sinner; and he who swears is as he who shuns an oath.* [3] *This is an evil in all that is done under the sun, that one fate comes to all; also the hearts of men are full of evil, and madness is in their hearts while they live, and after that they go to the dead.* [4] *But he who is joined with all the living has hope, for a living dog is better than a dead lion.* [5] *For the living know that they will die, but the dead know nothing, and they have no more reward; but the memory of them is lost.* [6] *Their love and their hate and their envy have already perished, and they have no more for ever any share in all that is done under the sun.*

7 *Go, eat your bread with enjoyment, and drink your wine with a merry heart; for God has already approved what you do.*

8 *Let your garments be always white; let not oil be lacking on your head.*

9 *Enjoy life with the wife whom you love, all the days of your vain life which he has given you under the sun, because that is your portion in life and in your toil at which you toil under the sun.* [10] *Whatever your hand finds to do, do it with your might; for there is no work or thought or knowledge or wisdom in Sheol, to which you are going.*

If we are right in introducing verse 2 with the words, *Everything before them is vanity* (1c), or, with NEB, 'Everything that confronts him, everything is empty',[2] the point will be that while our

---

he experiences). To me, the emphasis on God's inscrutability in 8:17, immediately before this verse, makes it more likely (and more relevant to the argument) that His attitude rather than man's is the issue here. *Cf.* RSV, NEB.

[2] The word 'vanity' in verse 1c of RSV (strictly 2a, MT), is found in the ancient versions but not in MT, which repeats 'everything' ('Everything before them is everything'). However, the consonants of 'everything' (*hkl*) and

surroundings give no clue to what God thinks of us, our prospects make it all too clear. To all appearances, God is just not interested. The things that are supposed to matter most to Him turn out to make no difference—or none that anyone can see—to the way we are disposed of in the end. Moral or immoral, religious or profane, we are all mown down alike. In a hundred years, as we say, it will all come to the same thing.

Yet while death seems to say this—and it has a way of getting the last word—we find ourselves stabbed into immediate protest. Qoheleth speaks for us all when he cries out, 'This is as wrong as anything that happens in this world' (3, TEV). What we may not notice, for he draws no attention to it here, is that this sense of outrage is just as much a fact about us as is our mortality. The fascination of this book throughout its length arises very largely from such collisions between obstinate facts of observation and equally obstinate intuitions. So it pushes us towards a synthesis which lies mostly beyond its own pages; in this case, the prospect of reward and punishment in the world to come.

Meanwhile we look at the world as it shows itself to us, with death as the universal obliterator and with evil running riot. The two things are not unrelated. To live in an apparently meaningless world is deeply disillusioning, and disillusion breeds destructiveness or despair—the *madness* of the violent or of the hopelessly withdrawn.

Is despair all that is left? Surprisingly enough, man in general thinks not, or the race would have perished long ago. And Qoheleth agrees. Life is decidedly worth living. After all, even at its worst, or near it, it is better than *nothing*, which is what death appears to be. The robust good sense of verse 4,[3] with its popular proverb to clinch the point, paves the way for a spirited refusal in the next two verses to let death browbeat the living before their time. Rather, let life put death to shame! Does the man alive know too much for comfort? But who would be a corpse and know nothing,[4] expect nothing, count for nothing in the world?

'vanity' (*hbl*) look so alike in Heb. that MT's puzzling repetition seems best explained as a copying error, either for 'vanity', as in RSV, or for the phrase 'everything is vanity' (*cf.* NEB).

[3] MT has 'he who is chosen' (√*bhr*), which yields little sense and appears to be a scribal error for 'joined' (√*hbr*), which is supported by LXX *et al.*

[4] Out of context, *the dead know nothing* (5) has sometimes been treated as a straight doctrinal statement. But even apart from the author's method, both

Under the very cloud of death, this life-affirming spirit lights up the rest of the passage (7–10), as far as anything temporal can; for though it is not the full answer, it does enjoy the approval of God. It is not for nothing that He is the source of all the gifts of earthly life: its bread and wine, festivity and work, marriage and love.

There are some striking resemblances between this passage (9:7–10) and some lines in the Epic of Gilgamesh, an Akkadian poem dating from the time of Abraham or earlier, which was widely known in the ancient world. At this point in its story the hero has been impelled by the death of his great friend to go in search of immortality, and has reached the garden of the gods. There the young woman Siduri, the wine-maker, speaks to him:

> 'Gilgamesh, whither are you wandering?
> Life, which you look for, you will never find.
> For when the gods created man, they let
> death be his share, and life
> withheld in their own hands.
> Gilgamesh, fill your belly—
> day and night make merry,
> let days be full of joy,
> dance and make music day and night.
> And wear fresh clothes,
> and wash your head and bathe.
> Look at the child that is holding your hand,
> and let your wife delight in your embrace.
> These things alone are the concern of men.'[5]

This is not the only place where sentiments of this kind are to be heard. From Egypt a funeral banquet song, perhaps roughly contemporary with Gilgamesh, contains this advice after reminding the living of what lies ahead of them:

'Follow thy desire, so long as thou livest. Put myrrh on thine head, clothe thee in fine linen, and anoint thee . . ., and vex not thine heart,—until that day of lamentation cometh to thee.'[6]

---

this statement and the next (*they have no more reward*) would clash with other scriptures if so taken. *Cf.*, *e.g.*, Lk. 16:23 ff.; 2 Cor. 5:10.

[5] The Epic of Gilgamesh, part of Tablet X, translated in H. Frankfort *et al.*, *Before Philosophy* (Pelican, 1949), p. 226.

[6] Translated in A. Erman, *The Literature of the Ancient Egyptians* (Methuen, 1927), p. 133.

A modern writer, however, has rightly pointed out the distinctive note that Qoheleth strikes, even when he writes in this key. 'For his counsels recommending an acceptance and enjoyment of the possible in every case contain a pointer to God', indeed to 'a positive will of God'.[7] This is particularly clear in the assurance of verse 7b that God has accepted the grateful gesture. That gesture is envisaged as not only grateful, but humble and eager, in the maxim, *do it with your might* (10); and at this point the brevity of life has become a spur, as it did for our Lord when He spoke of the onset of 'night . . . when no one can work' (Jn. 9:4). Yet it is characteristic of this book that even in this connection, death is introduced not with a passing glance but with a steady look at its desolating features.

But death is not the only hazard.

Changes and chances

9:11 *Again I saw that under the sun the race is not to the swift, nor the battle to the strong, nor bread to the wise, nor riches to the intelligent, nor favour to the men of skill; but time and chance happen to them all.* [12] *For man does not know his time. Like fish which are taken in an evil net, and like birds which are caught in a snare, so the sons of men are snared at an evil time, when it suddenly falls upon them.*

Time and chance are paired, no doubt because they both have a way of taking matters suddenly out of our hands. This is obvious enough where chance is concerned—for providence operates in secret, and to man's view life is largely made up of steps into the unknown and events out of the blue, any of which may change our whole pattern of existence in a moment. With regard to time, chapter 3 with its 'time to be born, . . . time to die', and so on, has already shown how relentlessly our lives are swung from one extreme to another by the tidal pull of forces we do not control. All this counterbalances the impression we may get from maxims about hard work, that success is ours to command. In the sea of life we are more truly the *fish . . . taken in an evil net*, or else unaccountably spared, than the masters of our fate and the captains of our souls.

The third thing to upset our calculations is presented to us

[7] G. von Rad, *Old Testament Theology* (English Tr., Oliver and Boyd, 1962), I, p. 457.

rather poignantly in the little parable of verses 13–16, and in the reflections which follow it to round off the chapter.

The fickleness of men

9:13 *I have also seen this example of wisdom under the sun, and it seemed great to me.* [14] *There was a little city with few men in it; and a great king came against it and besieged it, building great siegeworks against it.* [15] *But there was found in it a poor wise man, and he by his wisdom delivered the city. Yet no one remembered that poor man.* [16] *But I say that wisdom is better than might, though the poor man's wisdom is despised, and his words are not heeded.*

[17] *The words of the wise heard in quiet are better than the shouting of a ruler among fools.* [18] *Wisdom is better than weapons of war, but one sinner destroys much good.*

We can identify at once with the people in the *little city* under siege, and feel their relief when the amateur strategist—or is he a diplomatist?—brings off his masterstroke. If we are honest, we may still see ourselves in the last scene, when they totally forget him. But the parable is not a moral tale to show what people should do: it is a cautionary tale to show what they are like. If we are to identify with anybody, it is with the *poor wise man*—not as though we should fancy ourselves as universal consultants; simply that, sadly enough, we should learn not to count on anything as fleeting as public gratitude.

> 'Freeze, freeze, thou bitter sky,
> That dost not bite so nigh
> As benefits forgot:
> Though thou the waters warp,
> Thy sting is not so sharp
> As friend remember'd not.'[8]

In the pattern of the chapter this is one more example of what is unpredictable and cruel in life, to sap our confidence in what we can make of it on our own. The last two verses (17 f.) give an extra thrust to the parable by showing first how valuable and then how vulnerable is wisdom. We are left with more than a suspicion that in human politics the last word will regularly go to the loud voice of verse 17 or the cold steel of verse 18. Seldom to truth, seldom to merit.

[8] Shakespeare, *As You Like It*, Act II, Scene 7.

A third summary
A backward glance over
Ecclesiastes 7:1—9:18

Our author's calling, like Jeremiah's, could be summed up as

> 'to pluck up and to break down,
> to destroy and to overthrow,'

but then, and then only,

> 'to build and to plant'.[1]

By the end of chapter 9 he has made his case against our self-sufficiency. The first half of the book, whose progress we briefly recalled on pages 48 and 63, left us little reason for complacency, and the past three chapters have been sharpening the issues.

Unlike their predecessors, the proverbs and reflections in 7:1–22 brought us no respite from our main preoccupation, although we called them an interlude. With few exceptions the sayings were harsh (*e.g.*, 7:1-4); even, at one point, cynical (7:15–18); pushing the secularist hard up against the fact and implications (for him) of death. And when the argument was resumed in 7:23, it raised fresh doubts of human wisdom. Chapter 2 had already made the point that the wise man is as mortal as the fool; but now arose the pressing question, whether wisdom, in any serious sense, was attainable at all. Wise as a man might be in the many details of life (8:1-6; 9:13-18), it became clear that he would never find his way through to the heart of things, never even be sure that the truth, if he did discover it, would bear looking at. 'Who can find it out?' (7:24); 'who can tell him how it will be?' (8:7); 'whether it is love or hate man does not know' (9:1).

In other respects as well, the picture had darkened. Now there

---

[1] Je. 1:10.

were glimpses of moral turpitude: of injustice not only rampant but admired (8:10 f.), and of humanity not merely weak but 'fully set to do evil', pursuing its course with 'madness' (8:11; 9:3). And along with the ravages of death which had been emphasized throughout the book there emerged the hazards of time and chance (9:11 f.), to make further havoc of man's calculations.

Despite all this, there were a few gleams of better things, keeping some hope alive in us, to be fostered and justified in the remaining chapters. For at last Qoheleth has finished his work of demolition. The site has been cleared: he can turn to building and planting. Whether we regard the next chapter as the modest beginning of this process, or as an interlude to relieve the tension (comparable with 4:9—5:12 and 7:1-22), it will allow us to get our breath before reverting to the burning question of the book: whether life has any point, and if so, what it is.

For a start, then, there are matters of common sense for us to notice, which are as much a part of wisdom and sound living as are the questions we must face at the boundaries of our knowledge. We steady ourselves with reminders to be sensible (chapter 10), so that we may launch out more surely upon the call to be bold (11:1-6), joyful (11:7-10) and godly (chapter 12).

Ecclesiastes 10:1–20
Interlude: Be sensible!

This chapter takes a calm look at life, sampling it at random, so as to help us to keep our own standards high, without being too surprised at the oddities of others, or taken off our guard in our dealings with the powerful.

Folly

10:1 *Dead flies make the perfumer's ointment give off an evil odour;*
   so a little folly outweighs wisdom and honour.
2 *A wise man's heart inclines him toward the right,*
   but a fool's heart toward the left.
3 *Even when the fool walks on the road, he lacks sense,*
   and he says to every one that he is a fool.

Verse 1 puts into a vividly unpleasant form the principle on which the previous chapter ended: that it takes far less to ruin something than to create it. This, incidentally, is part of the advantage enjoyed by evil, and of its appeal to the vicious side of us; for to put it as bluntly as Qoheleth does, it is easier to make a stink than to create sweetness. But in this verse it is the sudden lapse or foolish impulse that is the trouble: and there are endless instances of prizes forfeited and good beginnings marred in a single reckless moment—not only by the irresponsible, such as Esau, but by the sorely tried, such as Moses and Aaron.

In verse 2 the modern versions are not happy with the dubious anatomy of AV, RV ('A wise man's heart is at his right hand . . .'). Perhaps JB puts it best, if freely: 'The wise man's heart leads him aright, the fool's heart leads him astray.' The right and left hands have always been widely viewed as lucky and unlucky, good and bad (*cf.* our use of the Latin word, *sinister*, 'left-hand'); and in our Lord's figure of the sheep and goats the two sides correspond to the two contrasted verdicts. But less decisively, there were also blessings of the right hand and of the left, differing in degree.[1] The fool, then, inclines to the less valuable, the less good and, by the same token, to the positively wrong. The preference shows in many ways: not only morally and spiritually. By contrast, the wise man's predilections are spelt out in the great list of 'whatevers' in Philippians 4:8.

Comedy breaks through in verse 3, as it has often done in Proverbs on this theme. To the practised eye of Qoheleth the fool has no way of disguising what he is,[2] except perhaps by total silence (*cf.* Pr. 17:28). Even then, his general bearing would probably give him away. But in fact he is too full of himself to refrain from airing his views to everyone he meets. To judge from Proverbs, his fine phrases will sound incongruous (Pr. 17:7), his tactless remarks impertinent (Pr. 18:6); and when you talk to him he is not really listening (Pr. 18:2). If he has a message for you he will get it wrong, and if he comes out with a sage remark it will misfire (Pr. 26:6 f.). You can fortunately sense his approach by the efforts of all and sundry to slip away (Pr. 17:12).

The social tightrope

10:4 *If the anger of the ruler rises against you, do not leave your place, for deference will make amends for great offences.*

5 *There is an evil which I have seen under the sun, as it were an error proceeding from the ruler:* 6 *folly is set in many high places, and the rich sit in a low place.* 7 *I have seen slaves on horses, and princes walking on foot like slaves.*

There is keen observation behind the quiet advice of verse 4, for what we are invited to notice is that rather absurd human phenomenon, the huff. If one can recognize its symptoms, one will be saved some self-inflicted damage—for while it may feel magnificent to 'resign your post' (NEB), ostensibly on principle but

---

[1] *Cf.* Ephraim and Manasseh, Gn. 48:13 ff.; see also Pr. 3:16.

[2] An alternative sense of 3b is grammatically possible, that he 'calls everyone else a fool' (NEB; but see NEB mg.). Commentators are divided on this, but most English translations agree with RSV rather than NEB.

actually in a fit of pride, it is in fact less impressive, more immature, than it feels. To be submissive to an autocratic master is not only the believer's duty (as the New Testament has taught us, 1 Pet. 2:18 ff.), but may also be his wisdom, since the anger that can be mollified by *deference* (4b) has itself the symptoms of a huff; and one person in that state is better than two.

Even worse, perhaps, than the autocrat is the weakling. With him in charge, anything can happen. The upheavals of verses 6 and 7 proceed *from the ruler* of verse 5, and they remind us how fragile our little hierarchies are. Yet every age gets taken by surprise. From ancient Egypt, many centuries before these words were written, come woebegone remarks sounding as topical to us as Qoheleth's:

'Why really, nobles are in lamentation, while poor men have joy . . .

'Why really, all maid-servants make free with their tongues. When their mistresses speak, it is burdensome to the servants . . . Behold, nobles' ladies are now gleaners, and nobles are in the workhouse.'[3]

If some are inclined to applaud, Qoheleth will not exactly quarrel with them—for his aim, throughout, is to shake our pathetic faith in the permanence of our affairs; and in any case he has no illusions about the men at the top.[4] But neither does he view these upsets as triumphs of social justice. The examples he has witnessed have been either turns of the wheel of fortune (7), or else appointments that went to the wrong people (*folly . . . set in many high places*, 6). We can make our own guess at the intrigues, threats, flatteries and bribes that paved the way for them.

Plain facts of life

10:8 *He who digs a pit will fall into it;*
     and a serpent will bite him who breaks through a wall.
 9 *He who quarries stones is hurt by them;*
     and he who splits logs is endangered by them.
 10 *If the iron is blunt, and one does not whet the edge,*
     he must put forth more strength;
     but wisdom helps one to succeed.

[3] 'The Admonitions of Ipu-wer', translated by John A. Wilson in *ANET*, pp. 441 f. Probably written before 2000 BC.
[4] *Cf.* 3:16; 4:1 ff., 13 ff.; 5:8 f.

¹¹ *If the serpent bites before it is charmed,*
there is no advantage in a charmer.

The outlook behind these pointed remarks is not fatalism, as verses 8 and 9 might suggest on their own,[5] but elementary realism. The blinding glimpse of the obvious in verse 10, backed up by the dry humour of the next verse, dispels any doubt. We are being urged to use our minds, and to look a little way ahead. For there are risks bound up with any vigorous action, and the person we call accident-prone has usually himself to blame, rather than his luck. He should have known; he could have taken care. But Qoheleth drops a hint of a parable by talking of *a pit* and of *a serpent*; for the pit that traps its maker was a proverbial picture of poetic justice,[6] and the unnoticed serpent was the very image of lurking retribution. This was how the prophet Amos saw it; so too did the witnesses of Paul's encounter with the viper.[7]

Verse 8, then, may be making a different point from verse 9, aimed at the unscrupulous rather than the feckless. As for the latter, they (or we?) are beautifully dealt with in verses 10 and 11: first with the elaborate patience suited to the dunce, then with a flash of wit and a touch of farce. After the startling opening, where the snake has been too quick for everybody, one can almost see the shrug that accompanies the throw-away line (NEB)—'the snake-charmer loses his fee'. As for the victim . . . but why labour the point?

Sense and nonsense

10:12 *The words of a wise man's mouth win him favour,*
but the lips of a fool consume him.
¹³ *The beginning of the words of his mouth is foolishness,*
and the end of his talk is wicked madness.
¹⁴ *A fool multiplies words,*
though no man knows what is to be,
and who can tell him what will be after him?

⁵ The assertions of verses 8 f. are generalizations, leaving exceptions and mere probabilities aside for the sake of a sharp outline. NEB legitimately renders them, 'may fall . . ., may be bitten', etc.; but it sacrifices a little of their forcefulness.
⁶ E.g., Pss. 7:15; 9:15; 35:7 f.; 57:6; etc.
⁷ Am. 5:18-20; 9:3; Acts 28:4.

> ¹⁵ *The toil of a fool wearies him,*
> *so that he does not know the way to the city.*

Words are naturally a favourite subject of the Wisdom writers, for they have an obvious place in the art of living; and it is the art rather than the object of life that dominates this chapter. But after a glance at the right use of words, we are faced at greater length with their misuse. Perhaps the proportion is a fair one.

To say (with RSV and most modern versions) that the words of a wise man *win him favour* (12) is only half the truth, though it makes a neat contrast to the second line. What is really said is that his words are 'grace'. Certainly this, which includes charm as well as kindness, wins favour if anything can; but at its best it is disinterested, and springs from the basic humility which is the beginning of wisdom.

The little portrait of the fool likewise hints at the inner attitudes that underlie his words. If we laughed at him in verse 3, we see the tragic and dangerous side of him now. In Scripture he is wrong-headed rather than dull: his thinking (and therefore his speaking) refuses to begin with God. Verse 13 in fact makes this clear, spanning the whole process from its foolish start to its disastrous end. That end, in *wicked madness*, may look too lurid to be true; but its two elements, moral and mental, are the final fruits of refusing the will and truth of God. If there are innumerable unbelievers whose earthly end could hardly be described as either wickedness or madness, it is only because the logic of their unbelief has not been followed through, thanks to the restraining grace of God. But when a whole society goes secular, the process is far more evident and thoroughgoing.

The neighbouring verses look at two features of a fool's talk. It is ill-judged, doing him no good (12), and ill-becoming, showing no diffidence in face of the unknown (14). While this is superficially the case with all of us in our foolish moments, it is true at a more serious level for the real fool, the ungodly man, whose whole way of speaking betrays his outlook (*cf.* Mt. 12:34-37), and whose confident opinions blithely disregard our human need of revelation.

Verse 15 is a tailpiece on the fool himself, but it would take a wise man to know exactly what it means! The second line is evidently a proverbial tag about the kind of person who gets the simplest of things wrong (*cf.* Is. 35:8)—he would get lost, we might say today, even if you put him on an escalator. This line is clearer without RSV's opening words (*so that*), and it could be more simply translated, '(one) who doesn't (even) know the way to town!' So the picture begins to emerge of a man who makes things needlessly difficult for himself by his stupidity. Just possibly there is a connection with the opinionated fool of the previous verse, making heavy weather of subjects that are quite beyond him; but more probably we are being shown just one more side of a foolish person's make-up. If so, it also suits the theme of the book, with its emphasis on the weariness of any labour that is pointless (*cf.*, *e.g.*, 1:8; 2:18-23), and we may need reminding that in the last analysis this is the thing that could make fools of us all. The book will end with a warning to the clever fool whose 'much study' only wears him out and diverts him from 'the end of the matter' (12:12 f.), which is the fear of God. To be ever learning, never arriving, as 2 Timothy 3:7 portrays some people, is to be a trifler who contrives to get lost on even the straightest *way to the city*. That is folly without even the excuse of ignorance.

Mostly about rulers

10:16 *Woe to you, O land, when your king is a child,*
and your princes feast in the morning!
17 *Happy are you, O land, when your king is the son of free men,*
and your princes feast at the proper time,
for strength, and not for drunkenness!
18 *Through sloth the roof sinks in,*
and through indolence the house leaks.
19 *Bread is made for laughter,*
and wine gladdens life,
and money answers everything.
20 *Even in your thought, do not curse the king,*
nor in your bedchamber curse the rich;
for a bird of the air will carry your voice,
or some winged creature tell the matter.

The chapter ends, as it began, with shrewd remarks on practical politics, as if to re-emphasize that the interest of the wise in ultimate questions does nothing to lessen their concern for the present. The wise man cares very much about the way his country is governed, and about the way to rule himself and his affairs, in a world which is at once demanding (18), delightful (19) and dangerous (20).

Verses 16 and 17 remind us of the influence that seeps down from the men at the top, to set the tone of a whole community. It can be true of the smallest units as well as the largest. The first picture shows a ruler without dignity or wisdom, surrounded by decadence; the second, a leader who is readily accepted, surrounded by responsible men. In case we should take either *child* or *free men* in these verses in too narrow a sense, an earlier passage has pointed out that age and status are not everything, even for kingship, and has spoken up for the young nobody who arrives with nothing in his favour but his gifts (4:13). The *child*, or 'lad', of verse 16 could indeed be a man in years, who has never grown up (*cf.* Is. 3:12), in contrast to, say, the young Josiah who 'while he was yet a boy . . . began to seek . . . God',[8] to the blessing of his country. And the mention of *free men*, or 'nobles', is not a touch of snobbery, only of political stability. They are not depicted in Scripture as paragons of virtue,[9] nor was an outstanding man like David or Jeroboam disqualified by not coming from their circle. The point of both verses is driven home by the prophecy of social breakdown in Isaiah 3:1-5, where the men of weight in the community were to be ousted,

> 'And I will make boys their princes,
> and babes shall rule over them . . .
> The youth will be insolent to the elder,
> and the base fellow to the honourable.'

As for decadent courtiers (16), Israel knew them well. The prophets paint faithful pictures of their day-long carousals (Is. 5:11, 22), their pampered idleness (Am. 6:4 ff.) and their descent into stupor and filth (Is. 28:7 f.). In such situations justice and truth are the nation's first casualties, 'fallen in the street' (Is. 59:14, AV).

It seems likely that the proverbs of verses 18 and 19 were placed here especially for their bearing on the ways of the powerful: their rule and misrule, their use and abuse of God's gifts, as seen

[8] 2 Ch. 34:3.
[9] They are spineless in 1 Ki. 21:8, 11; compromisers in Ne. 6:17 ff.; 13:17; and part of a disastrous regime in Je. 39:6.

in the previous verses. Then verse 20 will revert to these people more explicitly.

Certainly the *sloth* (18) which silently destroys a neglected house or a sluggish spirit, is as fatal to a kingdom as to a building or a person. Nothing else is needed to bring it down, and nothing is more devastating. Whatever kinds of damage can be safely overlooked, decay is not among them: time is on its side. In terms of the indolent officials castigated by the prophets in the passages we have noticed, their own decadence was to spread its rottenness to the very structure that sheltered them, until it collapsed over their heads.

In the proverb of verse 19, the first two lines may tie in with the feasting scenes, good and bad, that opened the paragraph (16 f.), but in any other context we should see them leading up to the punch-line about money. It need not be cynical: the point is not that every man has his price but that every gift has its use—and silver, in the form of money, is the most versatile of all. Our Lord made the same kind of point in Luke 16:9, and characteristically opened up a new vista as He did so. In its present setting, however, the proverb's first two lines may be meant to carry the chief weight, to make the point that to feast *for strength, and not for drunkenness* (17) is a happy thing, whereas excess is pointless. God's wholesome gifts are good, and their proper use delightful and perfectly sufficient.

With verse 20 we are back again explicitly with the men of power, including monetary power. (They will have their own way of taking verse 19c!) They are not comfortable company. To a twentieth-century reader there is something familiar in their too-sensitive ear for whispers, but they need no electronics for their espionage. They would not have reached their dizzy heights, or stayed there, without a sixth sense for dissidents.

Practical as ever, the writer sees this as a fact of life, and ends the chapter with advice on managing to live with it. To survive is the first step, even if it is by no means the last. Now he can lead us on towards the climax of the book.

Ecclesiastes 11:1—12:8
Towards home

The pace quickens now. The scene is unaltered: it has the same deep shadows and occasional highlights as before, but now we look at it resolutely rather than wistfully. We know the worst; so much the better: we can strike out in the right direction.

Three separate thrusts put us on the way towards 'the end of the matter'. We can summarize them in the headings we have chosen here for the three parts of these two remaining chapters: Be bold! Be joyful! Be godly!

Be bold!

11:1 *Cast your bread upon the waters,*
for you will find it after many days.
2 *Give a portion to seven, or even to eight,*
for you know not what evil may happen on earth.
3 *If the clouds are full of rain,*
they empty themselves on the earth;
and if a tree falls to the south or to the north,
in the place where the tree falls, there it will lie.
4 *He who observes the wind will not sow;*
and he who regards the clouds will not reap.
5 *As you do not know how the spirit comes to the bones in the womb of a woman with child, so you do not know the work of God who makes everything.*
6 *In the morning sow your seed, and at evening withhold not your hand; for you do not know which will prosper, this or that, or whether both alike will be good.*

This leads straight on from the sound advice of chapter 10, which we summed up in the words, 'Be sensible!' Caution had its place there; now it must give way to enterprise.

One of the frustrating things of life observed in 9:11 f. was the fact that time and chance can overturn our finest plans. If that can be a paralysing thought, it can also be a spur to action: for if there are risks in everything, it is better to fail in launching out than in hugging one's resources to oneself. We already catch a breath of the New Testament blowing through the first two verses, a hint of our Lord's favourite paradox that 'he who loves his life loses it', and that 'the measure you give will be the measure you get'.[1] This will be true, in one degree or another, whether Qoheleth is speaking here of business ventures or of plain generosity—for it is difficult to be sure which of these he chiefly means,[2] or whether he speaks first of one, then of the other.

The thought of verses 3 and 4 brings together again the things we can do nothing about and those that call for firm decision and action. The two examples given here—the clouds which follow their own laws and times, not ours, and the fallen tree which has consulted no-one's convenience—may start us thinking of may-be's and might-have-beens; but our business is to grapple with what actually is, and what lies within reach. Few great enterprises have waited for ideal conditions; no more should we. Then verse 5 relates the realm of the unknown and unknowable to *God who makes everything*. The example it has chosen is one of His crowning works, one on which all our questioning and thinking depends: the marvel of the human body and the human spirit. Did our Lord have this verse in mind when He spoke to Nicodemus of the second birth? Like Qoheleth, He made good use of the fact that a single word serves in the biblical languages for the *wind* (4) and the *spirit* (5),[3] and He seized on the same points: their hiddenness and freedom from our control, but their potent reality none the less.

[1] Jn. 12:25; Mt. 7:2.
[2] 'Send' (not *Cast*, which is misleading) suggests trade, whether *bread* stands for grain or for one's livelihood. Likewise verse 2 with its reference to an uncertain future has often been likened to our saying against putting all our eggs in one basket. On the other hand, *bread* is the appropriate gift to the hungry (though usually they are envisaged as local, not beyond the seas), and the risk of hard times (2b) could well be an argument for giving liberally while you can. *Cf.* Acts 11:27-30; 2 Cor. 9:6 ff.; Gal. 6:7 ff.
[3] *Cf.* Jn. 3:8.

Verse 6, clinching the passage, has a buoyancy of spirit which again reminds us of the atmosphere of the New Testament. The true response to uncertainty is a redoubling of effort, 'making the most of the time', 'urgent in season and out of season', expressed by Qoheleth in terms of the farmer and his work, and by Paul in terms of the spiritual harvest from the good seed of the gospel and of works of mercy.[4]

It is a stimulating call, with no thought of faltering, yet no trace of bravado or irresponsibility. The very smallness of our knowledge and control, the very likelihood of hard times (2b), so frequently impressed on us throughout the book, become the reasons to bestir ourselves and show some spirit. In this frame of mind we can now turn to the delights of life, the subject of the next few verses, not as if they were opiates to tranquillize us, but as invigorating gifts of God.

Be joyful!

11:7 *Light is sweet, and it is pleasant for the eyes to behold the sun.*

8 *For if a man lives many years, let him rejoice in them all; but let him remember that the days of darkness will be many. All that comes is vanity.*

9 *Rejoice, O young man, in your youth, and let your heart cheer you in the days of your youth; walk in the ways of your heart and the sight of your eyes. But know that for all these things God will bring you into judgment.*

10 *Remove vexation from your mind, and put away pain from your body; for youth and the dawn of life are vanity.*

Candid as ever, these verses match the delight of existence with the seriousness of it. Each joy here is confronted by its opposite or its complement; there is no softening of the colours on either side. The bliss of being alive is captured in the lovely sentence which opens with the saying, *Light is sweet . . .* (7); and this youthful radiance may last, as verse 8a points out, to the end. But not beyond. The author has not gone back on his insistence that, by themselves, time and all things temporal will disappoint us, who have eternity in our hearts (*cf.* 3:11). Their light must give way to *the days of darkness* and the undoing of everything

---

[4] *Cf.* Eph. 5:16; 2 Tim. 4:2 f.; 2 Cor. 8:2; 9:6.

under the sun; and we must face the fact or else be shattered by it. Joy needs no pretences to enhance it; but how it can survive in face of death and the frustrations of the world is a secret which only the next chapter will begin to unfold.

⊁ Meanwhile verse 9 reminds us of another aspect of joy: its relation to what is right. At first sight this reminder of judgment looks like a sword of Damocles hanging over us, to rob the feast of all its relish. It can be that to us, but only if our joy is a parody of its true self. *The ways of your heart and the sight of your eyes*—or, in two words, perfect freedom—must have a goal worth reaching, a 'Well done!' to strive for, to find fulfilment. Otherwise triviality takes over, or worse still, vice. Whichever of these connotations the word 'playboy' has for us, we know that for lack of relating his life to anything demanding, still less to heaven's assessment, that man is a pitiable figure. So this verse, by insisting that our ways matter to God and are therefore meaningful through and through, robs joy of nothing but its hollowness.

As I see it, verse 10 follows up this line of thought. At a first glance it may seem no better than escapism: a desperate attempt to squeeze some pleasure out of a pointless situation. But it makes more sense[5] if it is enlarging on the invitation to the 'young man' of verse 9 to rejoice indeed in his youth, but to rejoice responsibly. To idolize the state of youth and to dread the loss of it is disastrous: it spoils the gift even while we have it. To see it, instead, as a passing phase, 'beautiful in its time' but not beyond it, is to be free from its frustrations. The *vexation* which is spoken of in this verse meets us more than once in the book as the bitterness provoked by a hard and disappointing world.[6] It has its place in making realists of us, as 7:3 points out; but that gives us no reason to be pessimists. At its very opening, this verse banishes depression; and the second line, *put away pain from your body*, may well be a reinforcing echo of the first, after the style of Hebrew poetry. But it may be carrying the thought a step further, into the moral realm, since the word translated *pain* means basically 'evil'.[7] If so, it will chime in with the reminder that

[5] Note the relation between the two clauses: the second gives the reason for the first.

[6] See 1:18; 2:23; 7:3 (Heb.).

[7] This is no more than a possibility, for it is often morally neutral (*cf.* 12:1). Yet the call to 'put away evil from thy flesh' (AV, RV) makes a most fitting preparation for the last line: *for youth and the dawn of life are vanity.*

all our ways are of concern to God who judges us (9c). Joy was created to dance with goodness, not alone.

But the positive approach to life which has dominated this chapter must rest on something more substantial than cheerfulness or courage, or even sound morality. The final chapter gives itself to what is basic, and urges us to lose no time in making it our business too.

Be godly!

12:1 *Remember also your Creator in the days of your youth, before the evil days come, and the years draw nigh, when you will say, 'I have no pleasure in them';* **2** *before the sun and the light and the moon and the stars are darkened and the clouds return after the rain;* **3** *in the day when the keepers of the house tremble, and the strong men are bent, and the grinders cease because they are few, and those that look through the windows are dimmed,* **4** *and the doors on the street are shut; when the sound of the grinding is low, and one rises up at the voice of a bird, and all the daughters of song are brought low;* **5** *they are afraid also of what is high, and terrors are in the way; the almond tree blossoms, the grasshopper drags itself along and desire fails; because man goes to his eternal home, and the mourners go about the streets;* **6** *before the silver cord is snapped, or the golden bowl is broken, or the pitcher is broken at the fountain, or the wheel broken at the cistern,* **7** *and the dust returns to the earth as it was, and the spirit returns to God who gave it.* **8** *Vanity of vanities, says the Preacher; all is vanity.*

At last we are ready—if we ever intend to be—to look beyond earthly vanities to God, who made us for Himself. The title *Creator* [8] is well chosen, reminding us from earlier passages in the book that He alone sees the pattern of existence whole (3:11); that His was the workmanship we have spoilt by our 'devices' (7:29); and that His creativity is continuous and unsearchable (11:5). For our part, to *remember* Him is no perfunctory or purely mental act· it is to drop our pretence of self-sufficiency and commit ourselves to Him. Such at least is what, in Scripture, it de-

---

[8] TEV has been too subtle in suggesting a punning allusion to 'your grave', a word similar in sound, but not in spelling, to *Creator* (cf. Scott). That word never has the possessive ('your', *etc.*) except when it is used in its primary sense of a well or cistern. For discussion of other over-ingenious suggestions, see the commentaries.

mands of man in his pride or his extremity.[9] At its best and strongest, remembrance can be a matter of passionate fidelity, a loyalty as intense as the psalmist's towards his homeland:

> 'Let my tongue cleave to the roof of my mouth,
>   if I do not remember you,
> If I do not set (you)
>   above my highest joy!'[1]

When remembrance means as much as this, there can be no half measures or temporizing. Youth and the whole span of life are not too much to pour into it. It is in this spirit that we are made to face once more the fact of our mortality. This is the last and longest treatment of it. At the same time it is one of the most beautiful of all sequences of word-pictures by this master of language: a supreme fulfilment of his twofold ambition, 'to find pleasing words', and 'words of truth' (10).

At the beginning and end of this passage he writes directly, without metaphors. We hear the very accents of old age in the regretful words, *'I have no pleasure in them'* (1), and in verse 7 we are reminded of God's sentence upon Adam: 'to dust you shall return.' But between these points there is a profusion of images, some of which will conjure up with utmost vividness some aspect of ageing or dying, while others tease us by allusions that at this distance we can scarcely catch—thereby awakening in us either the poet or the pedant.

It should be the poet, or at least the listener to poetry. If some obscurities in these lines can be clarified, so much the better for kindling our imagination; but so much the worse if they tempt us into treating this graceful poem as a laboured cryptogram, or forcing every detail into a single rigid scheme.

There is the chill of winter in the air of verse 2, as the rains persist and the clouds turn daylight into gloom, and then night into pitch blackness. It is a scene sombre enough to bring home to us not only the fading of physical and mental powers but the more general desolations of old age. There are many lights that are liable then to be withdrawn, besides those of the senses and faculties, as, one by one, old friends are taken, familiar customs change, and long-held hopes now have to be abandoned. All this will come at a stage when there is no longer the resilience of

[9] Dt. 8:17, 18; Jon. 2:7.
[1] Ps. 137:6.

youth or the prospect of recovery to offset it. In one's early years, and for the greater part of life, troubles and illnesses are chiefly set-backs, not disasters. One expects the sky to clear eventually. It is hard to adjust to the closing of that long chapter: to know that now, in the final stretch, there will be no improvement: the clouds will always gather again, and time will no longer heal, but kill.

So it is in youth, not age, that these inexorable facts are best confronted, when they can drive us into action—that total response to God which was the subject of verse 1—not into despair and vain regrets.

In verses 3 and 4a the picture changes.[2] Now it is no longer one of nightfall, storm and winter, but of a great house in decline. Its former glories of power, style, liveliness and hospitality can now be surmised only by contrast with their few, pathetic relics. In the brave struggle to survive there is almost a more pointed reminder of decay than in a total ruin. It is still part of our own scene; our own future is facing us and we cannot avoid involvement with this foretaste of it.

That picture, to my mind, is best taken in its entirety, not laboriously broken down into the constituent metaphors for human arms, legs, teeth, and so on, which doubtless underlie it— as though the poet had expressed himself inadequately. The dying house reveals us to ourselves as no mere catalogue or inventory could.

With the second half of verse 4, however, the method changes, though not the mood. There is no longer a single scheme, but separate, particular metaphors, which therefore call for individual study.

In verse 4b, NEB finds two expressions of deafness: 'when the chirping of the sparrow grows faint and the song-birds fall silent.' But the first of these is not supported by the Hebrew or the Greek, which suggest rather an old man's early waking.[3]

---

[2] Some, however, would find a single frame of reference throughout the poem: e.g., an anatomical allegory from first to last; or an impression of winter, storm or nightfall as they affect the world of nature and the activities of men; or an account of a household going into mourning on the death of its master. For discussions of these theories, see the larger commentaries.

[3] With his deafness he will hardly be wakened or startled by the sparrow, but perhaps the phrase is simply a note of time, like our 'up with the lark'. The Heb. would also allow, just possibly, the sense, 'He (i.e., his voice) rises into a sparrow's voice'; but it would be an awkward way of putting it.

Song-birds, however, may well be the meaning of *daughters of song*, as the Hebrew puts it; and it makes little difference to the sense whether we take it this way or as meaning individual songs or notes of music. With old age, these cheerful evidences of a living world about us grow remote and faint; one feels no longer fully part of it.

Verse 5 adds new touches to the picture, first by its observation of an old man's fear of falling or being jostled, now that he is unsteady and slow-moving; then by its little cluster of thought-provoking metaphors; finally by its glimpse of a funeral in progress. As for the metaphors, the white hair of age is vividly suggested by the *almond tree* which has exchanged the dark colours of winter for its head of pale blossom. The unnaturalness of the old man's slow, stiff walk, a parody of the suppleness and spring of youth, is brought out by the incongruous sight of a *grasshopper*— that embodiment of lightness and agility—slowed down to a laborious crawl [4] by damage or by the cold. The third metaphor is conveniently interpreted for us in RSV (*cf.* AV) in the words, *and desire fails*—for this is the point of the Hebrew expression, 'the caper-berry fails'. This berry was highly regarded as a stimulus to appetite and as an aphrodisiac. The reply of the aged Barzillai to David's offer of a place at court has often been quoted for its aptness to this whole context: 'I am this day eighty years old; can I discern what is pleasant and what is not? Can your servant taste what he eats or what he drinks? Can I still listen to the voice of singing men and singing women?' [5]

So, at the end of this verse (5), the flow of metaphors is interrupted by plain speaking of the end of man's journey, and of the last, ineffectual services his friends can perform for him. The expression, *his eternal home*, speaks here only of finality; not of the Christian's prospect of 'a house not made with hands, eternal in the heavens' (2 Cor. 5:1).

Most memorably of all, the pictures of verse 6 capture the beauty and fragility of the human frame: a masterpiece as delicately wrought as any work of art, yet as breakable as a piece of earthenware, and as useless in the end as a broken wheel. The first half of this verse seems to portray a golden lamp suspended

---

[4] This follows RSV's interpretation (*drags itself along*) of a verb which means either 'burdens itself' or 'becomes a burden'. If the latter is meant (*cf.* AV, RV, RSV mg.), the point will be that the lightest load is heavy to the aged.
[5] 2 Sa. 19:35.

by a silver chain; it will take only the snapping of a link to let it fall and be spoilt. And if this seems too finely-drawn a picture of our familiar selves, it is balanced by the scene at the deserted well —eloquent of the transience of the simplest, most basic things we do. There will be a last time for every familiar journey, every routine job.

There is a reminder in verse 7 of the tragedy behind this sequence: the fatal choice which led up to the sentence:

> 'You are dust,
> and to dust you shall return.'[6]

It is not this writer's only allusion to the fall of man: he has already put the blame for our condition where it belongs, in his dictum of 7:29: 'God made man upright, but they have sought out many devices.' And if, to our ears, there is a hopeful ring to the ending of verse 7, ... *and the spirit returns to God who gave it*, we are almost certainly hearing more than he intends. He has earlier raised the question of an after-life, and refused to be drawn.[7] This latest saying need mean no more than what is said about men and animals alike in Psalm 104:29; 'When thou hidest thy face, they are dismayed; when thou takest away their breath,[8] they die and return to their dust.' In other words, life is not at our command. The body will revert to its own elements, and the breath of life was always God's to give, and God's to take away.

So in verse 8, with the experience of the whole book behind us, and finally with this chapter's haunting pictures of mortality to enforce the point, we come back to the initial cry, *Vanity of vanities*, and find it justified. Nothing in our search has led us home; nothing that we are offered under the sun is ours to keep.

But we are forgetting the context. This very passage points us beyond anything 'under the sun', in the words, *your Creator*, and it invites response to Him. It also points us to the present, as the time of opportunity. Death has not yet reached out to us: let it rattle its chains at us and stir us into action!

---

[6] See Gn. 3.

[7] 3:21.

[8] Lit. 'their spirit'. It is the same word as in our present verse.

Ecclesiastes 12:9–14
Conclusion

The thinker as teacher

12:9 *Besides being wise, the Preacher also taught the people knowledge, weighing and studying and arranging proverbs with great care.* 10 *The Preacher sought to find pleasing words, and uprightly he wrote words of truth.*

We stand back for a moment to see the person and the process behind this remarkable book. The opening remarks point out the partnership between thought and expression, research and teaching, which the book itself has illustrated. We have seen how well the chapters of practical advice balance and supplement the probing reflections which they interrupt. What emerges in the rest of these two verses is the store the author sets on his calling as teacher. He is not the proud thinker who has no time for lesser minds: rather, he accepts the challenging ideal of perfect clarity. As verse 10 points out, it will take the skill and integrity, the charm and courage, of an artist and a scholar to do justice to the task. On the strength of that single verse, this man should be the patron saint of writers.

Teachings with a point

12:11 *The sayings of the wise are like goads, and like nails firmly fixed are the collected sayings which are given by one Shepherd.* 12 *My son, beware of anything beyond these. Of making many books there is no end, and much study is a weariness of the flesh.*

Here then are two more qualities that mark the pointed sayings of the wise: they spur the will and stick in the memory. With this, Qoheleth, master as he is, pays unwitting tribute to the greatest wisdom-teacher of all: our Lord, whose sayings have both these marks supremely, just as they also excel by the criterion of verse 10, as 'pleasing words' and 'words of truth'. They marry felicity with fearlessness: partners which should not be put asunder.

What matters above all is that these are words of authority. For all their variety and evident humanity, they are *given* to the wise. They are a unity, and they are from God. This second term for God, the *one Shepherd*, is a welcome complement to the majestic title in verse 1, 'your Creator'. The God 'afar off', whose writ runs everywhere, is equally the God 'at hand',[1] who knows and can be known, who speaks to us with man's voice and yet with finality.

Curiously enough, as verse 12 perceives, this may not suit us. We grow addicted to research itself, in love with our hard questions. An answer would spoil everything. C. S. Lewis, in one of the confrontations in *The Great Divorce*, captures the very tone and temper of this attitude, at the stage when it has taken final hold of a man. In that scene, on the borders of heaven, a lifelong 'searcher' is being invited in. He is told:

'I can promise you . . . no scope for your talents: only forgiveness for having perverted them. No atmosphere of inquiry, for I will bring you to the land not of questions but of answers, and you shall see the face of God.'

'Ah, but we must all interpret those beautiful words in our own way! For me there is no such thing as a final answer. The free wind of inquiry must *always* continue to blow through the mind, must it not?' . . .

. . . 'Listen!' said the White Spirit. 'Once you were a child. Once you knew what inquiry was for. There was a time when you asked questions because you wanted answers, and were glad when you had found them. Become that child again: even now.'

'Ah, but when I became a man I put away childish things.'[2]

No argument, no appeal will avail against this infinite elasticity. The encounter, already fruitless, ends with the gentle sophist's remembering an appointment, making his apologies, and hurrying off to his discussion group in hell.

[1] *Cf.* Je. 23:23 f.
[2] C. S. Lewis, *The Great Divorce* (Bles, 1945), pp. 40 f.

The point of arrival

13 *The end of the matter; all has been heard. Fear God, and keep his commandments; for this is the whole duty of man.* 14 *For God will bring every deed into judgment, with every secret thing, whether good or evil.*

So far, all our paths have come to nothing. They have lost themselves long before we could get within reach of anything eternal and absolute. But the path on which this chapter has set us is pointing to God. Here is the goal we were made for: the Eternal towards whom the 'eternity in man's mind' (*cf.* 3:11) was meant to home and gravitate.

If this way of putting it calls attention to man's need rather than God's demand, these two verses will soon redress the balance. But they gladly give the human element its due, in the words, *for this is the whole of man.* True, it is among other things his whole duty; but the Hebrew does not say so: it leaves this wholeness undefined. 'This', as we might translate it, 'is all that there is to man'; but it is an 'all' which stands in utter contrast to the 'vanity' with which the book has been confronting us. Here at last we shall find reality, and find ourselves.

Not, however—and with this the balance is restored—not as perfectionists seeking what is best for them, but as servants reporting to their proper master. *Fear God* is a call that puts us in our place, and all other fears, hopes and admirations in their place.

The last verse of all drives home the point just made, with a final blow that is sharp enough to hurt, but shrewd enough to jolt us out of apathy. It kills complacency to know that nothing goes unnoticed and unassessed, not even the things that we disguise from ourselves. But at the same time it transforms life. If God cares as much as this, nothing can be pointless.

This is the truth already put to us in 11:9; and what is more, it colours all the teaching of Christ, to whom no detail on earth could be too small to matter in heaven—an idle word, the death of a sparrow, a cup of cold water, the repentance of one sinner. It was this, too, that spurred Paul on to be 'urgent in season and out of season' and to finish his course with joy. For any other master, or for none,

> 'The peoples toil—only for the fire,
> And the nations weary themselves—all for nothing'.[3]

[3] Hab. 2:13, as translated by J. H. Eaton (*Torch Bible Commentaries*, SCM Press, 1961).

It is a very different thing to be under a master to whom the worker and the work both matter deeply, and whose judgment is unerring.

It was no part of our author's task to enquire further into this judgment: how and when it would find expression. There is a place for that. But there is a place—it is here—for the silence which draws attention to the bare fact of God's approval or displeasure. When every detail has been filled in, this is still the crux. On this, and nothing else at all, turns the question whether 'all things are yours' (as Paul puts it, going on to specify 'the world . . . life . . . death . . . the present . . . the future')[4] or, beyond remedy, 'all is vanity'.

[4] 1 Cor. 3:21 f.

Part Three

WHAT ARE WE TO SAY TO THIS?

—an epilogue

THE Christian can add his Amen to this voice from the Old Testament. Our author was brief; we can follow his example. A confession, a poem, a prayer, and one of Paul's great perorations, will be words enough to end with.

The confession is Augustine's: almost too familiar to repeat, yet it might have been written as a coda to this very book, instead of as a prelude to his own story:

> Thou hast made us for thyself,
> and our heart is restless till it rests in thee.

The poem is by George Herbert, its aptness becoming more and more apparent towards its perfect close:

> When God at first made man,
> Having a glass of blessing standing by;
> Let us (said He) pour on him all we can:
> Let the world's riches, which dispersèd lie,
>   Contract into a span.
>
>   So strength first made a way;
> Then beauty flowed, then wisdom, honour, pleasure.
> When almost all was out, God made a stay,
> Perceiving that alone of all His treasure,
>   Rest, in the bottom lay.
>
>   For if I should (said He)
> Bestow this jewel also on My creature,
> He would adore My gifts instead of Me,

And rest in nature, not the God of nature:
  So both should losers be.

Yet let him keep the rest,
But keep them with repining restlessness:
Let him be rich and weary, that at least,
If goodness lead him not, yet weariness
  May toss him to My breast.

The prayer was written by William Laud:

Grant, O Lord, that we may live in thy fear,
die in thy favour, rest in thy peace,
rise in thy power, reign in thy glory;
for thine own beloved Son's sake,
Jesus Christ our Lord.

The peroration is from 1 Corinthians 15:54, 58, that final answer to the cry of 'Vanity!'

When the perishable puts on the imperishable, and the mortal puts on immortality, then shall come to pass the saying that is written:
  'Death is swallowed up in victory.'

Therefore, my beloved brethren, be steadfast, immovable, always abounding in the work of the Lord, knowing that in the Lord your labour is not in vain.